SUPER CONFIDENCE

By the same author

ASSERT YOURSELF

SUPER CONFIDENCE

The woman's guide to getting what you want out of life

Gael Lindenfield

THORSONS PUBLISHING GROUP

First published 1989

© Gael Lindenfield 1989

Illustrations by Jessica Stockham

British Library Cataloguing in Publication Data

Lindenfield, Gael
Super Confidence:
the woman's guide to getting what you want
out of life.
1. Women, Self-development
I. Title
158'.1'024042

ISBN 0-7225-1870-6

Thorsons Publishing Group,
Wellingborough, Northamptonshire NN8 2RQ, England.

Printed and Bound in Great Britain by
Hartnolls Limited, Bodmin, Cornwall.

3 5 7 9 10 8 6 4 2

Contents

I would like to dedicate this book to Britta Harding, whose remarkable talents as a therapist gave me my first glimpse of my own potential and whose equally remarkable qualities as a friend have given me invaluable support and encouragement throughout my struggle to realize it.

Acknowledgements

The ideas contained in this programme have been developed through a 'trial and error' process, over several years. I am indebted to the many hundreds of people who have attended my courses and given me the honest and constructive criticism which has now enabled me to write this book with confidence! I would particularly like to mention my many friends at MIND YOUR SELF in Leeds, many of whom I originally knew as my 'clients' and who now work alongside me as talented and creative counsellors.

I would also like to thank my husband, Stuart, for his never-ending support and very practical midnight editing skills.

Finally, I am grateful to my daughters, Susie and Laura, who have been content to accept periods of 'not-so-perfect' mothering during the final stages in the preparation of this book.

Introduction

We often talk about confidence as though it were something that Fairy Godmothers bring. We may say, for example, 'She's lucky, she's got bags of confidence.' But are we so sure that we know what we mean when we use the word 'confidence'? Have we ever looked inside those mysterious 'bags' to see just what they *do* contain? Is it really up to 'luck' whether we possess this prized quality or not? If so, are men – and some women – just 'born lucky'? If not, how do you go about filling those 'bags' when they feel so uncomfortably empty?

These are just some of the questions which this book plans to discuss, and to answer.

When, several years ago, I first started running confidence-building workshops, I felt quite anxious. Would people expect me to be the supreme model of confidence? I was only too aware of a number of areas in my life where I was still struggling to maintain a feeling of confidence. I had to remind myself that being confident is not the same as being perfect! I had, once again, to look back at myself as I was in my twenties, in order to remind myself of the gigantic strides forward I had made during the previous 10 to 15 years, and I had to reappraise how this had been achieved. I am not prepared to give the credit for this achievement to Lady Luck because it rightly belongs to myself and to a number of other people who have guided and supported me through these years of growth. This book is an attempt to share what I have gained from this personal learning experience, as well as the knowledge I have acquired as a therapist in helping others to build up *their* own confidence.

She's lucky, she's got bags of confidence

The book is divided into four sections. Section one looks at the different elements of confidence. I will discuss the theory behind the belief that these elements can be nurtured and developed at any age.

Section two concentrates on inner confidence and looks at the importance of establishing a sound foundation for confident behaviour by improving our self-knowledge and self-esteem.

Section three outlines the skills we need to learn and develop, in order to behave confidently and establish effective and fulfilling relationships in a wide range of situations.

Section four introduces a series of exercises which can be used as the basis of a confidence-building programme for use by both individuals working on their own and self-help groups.

This book is not intended to be digested at thriller-reading speed; it is essentially a workbook, so read it a chapter at a time. Give yourself time to think, observe, and discuss before moving on, so that you can relate its contents to your personal experiences. This book does not offer an instant miracle cure for lack of confidence, but it can guide you along a well-trodden path which has led hundreds of people to a more exciting and enriching life.

Chapter 1

Understanding confidence

If we would like to be more confident, the first step we must take is to conjure a picture in our minds of the kind of person we would like to be.

How do we recognize a confident woman?

We will notice that a confident woman is behaving as though:

- **She loves herself** – and she doesn't mind us knowing that she cares for herself

- **She understands herself** – and continues to wonder about herself as she grows and develops

- **She knows what she wants** – and is not afraid to keep setting new goals for herself

- **She thinks positively** – and doesn't feel overwhelmed by problems

- **She behaves skilfully** – and knows which behaviour is appropriate for each individual situation.

We tend to feel good in the company of a confident woman because:

- We feel secure because we know where we stand with her. She is open and genuine. If she is feeling good, she lets us know; if she is feeling cross or anxious, she will also let us know. We do not have to worry about what she might be thinking about us, or about the situation we are in

- She doesn't depend on 'putting down' other people in order to feel powerful, so we can more easily trust that she will be fair and will not abuse us

- She will encourage confidence in us because she prefers the company of confident people

- She does not set herself up as being perfect and is always willing to acknowledge her own weaknesses and mistakes

- She is often lively because her energy is precious to her and she uses it selectively and with great care

- She can also be peaceful and relaxed because she does not feel she constantly has to prove herself through her words and actions

- She will give us a sense of optimism, because she will think creatively about problems rather than spending hours moaning about them.

What is the price we pay for lack of confidence?

There are very few people who haven't experienced the pain and disappointment which accompanies lack of confidence, but let's take a moment to remind ourselves of the price we can pay. The following list will probably jog some memories for most of us.

We feel:

- Isolated and lonely
- Acutely embarrassed and awkward

- Frightened and powerless
- Physically sick and tense
- In awe of confident people
- Worthless, useless and insignificant
- Guilty and to blame
- Pessimistic; that there's no point in trying
- Depressed and apathetic
- Misunderstood
- Let down because we see life passing us by
- Resentful and embittered.

In some people these feelings may be obvious, in others they may be well-concealed under a brash veneer of apparent success and self-confidence. As a therapist, I have been in the privileged position of hearing many people reveal these kinds of feelings for the first time to anyone. Many people do not admit them to themselves until they face a crisis which confronts them with the reality of their life; often this crisis is their impending death, when life is literally about to pass them by. Perhaps some people are satisfied with the hope that their life on earth may reap them rewards in the Kingdom of Heaven, but the majority of us want more out of this life.

> *It's going to be fun to watch and see how long the meek can keep the earth after they inherit it.*
> Kim Hubbard, *Abe Martin's Sayings*, (1915)

Can you be too confident?

Many women openly acknowledge to me that they are frightened of embarking on a confidence-building programme because they are afraid of becoming 'over-confident'. They have, perhaps, been carrying around an image in their heads of certain women they have known and not liked, even though they may secretly have admired and envied those women's success. They give me examples of head girls at school, bosses at work, politicians and film stars. To prove their point, they often delight in telling me stories of how these people ended up being alone and unhappy. The moral of these tales is that, if you 'get too big for your boots', you will lose out in the end. But I see this as an irrelevant argument, because being confident isn't about being 'too big for your boots' – it is about learning to get the boots that fit and to keep changing the boots as you get bigger!

So perhaps we should spend some time debunking some of those outdated, stereotyped myths about confident women. Much of the confusion arises because people are often not very clear about the differences between assertive and aggressive behaviour. We shall discuss these differences later but, for the moment, let's remember that, until relatively recently, neither of these behaviours have been used much by the average woman. So, when we see a woman behaving differently, even though we may admire her, we will tend at first to feel uncomfortable. When we feel discomfort we tend also to begin to feel fearful and suspicious. We will feel even more strongly if we are anxious about changing our own behaviour.

So the chain of 'events' inside our heads may go something like this:

I notice a woman behaving differently
↓
I feel uncomfortable
↓
I feel anxious
↓
I become suspicious of her behaviour
↓
I begin to look for a negative interpretation of
what she is doing and saying
↓
I comfort myself with the thought that it wouldn't
be a good idea to be like her, after all!

We must remind ourselves that a confident woman is not:

- **Bossy** – especially just for the sake of being bossy. She is prepared to lead authoritatively when she knows she has the skills to do so. She is also willing and able to delegate responsibility because she does not feel threatened by being led by other people, if it is appropriate that they should do so

- **Selfish** – She is aware that in order to help other people, firstly you must know how to help yourself and, secondly, you must know how to look after yourself, so that you have the time and energy to be useful to others in need

- **A 'know-all'** – One of the reasons for her confidence is that she has the ability to realize her limitations and is not afraid to acknowledge them

- **Unfeminine** – She delights in being a woman and doesn't feel the need to 'be like a man', in appearance or behaviour, in order to be successful. She is able to have egalitarian relationships with both men and women

- **'Frigid'** – She loves and accepts her body's feelings and desires. She acknowledges her need for warmth and intimacy and doesn't fear that she will lose control if she lets herself be spontaneous

- **A loner** – even though she may often enjoy her own company. She has good relationships because she is able to take risks and make demands within them and she is confident that she will not fall apart totally if she is rejected. She may have fewer 'friends' than an unconfident person because she is selective and does not waste her energy trying to please lots of acquaintances

- **Inevitably rich** – In our culture, unfortunately, success is often measured in economic terms. Although it is true that money can buy you a few confidence boosters and some of the trappings that make you look confident, you only have to read some of the autobiographies of the rich to see that wealth doesn't give you any guarantees

- **Highly successful** – especially in the field of work. Many more women are now working and, in the course of their work, meet the temptation to follow the traditional masculine code of 'proving yourself through work'. A sign

Babies show no sign of doubting their rights

of a confident woman may be that she chooses to do just the opposite! She may be quite content to stay at the bottom of the ladder or only climb halfway up, even if she is aware of her potential to get to the top.

Are we born confident?

Well, until someone shows me a baby who is not confident, I will remain convinced that we are! Babies show no signs of doubting their rights to get what they want and they will stretch to their limits to get what they want and need. Freud, the great father of psychology, used the phrase 'His majesty, the baby'. Any of us who has experienced looking after babies, male or female, knows just what he means!

Our inheritance

Freud, as most people know, was one of the first people to make us aware of how important our childhood experiences are in forming our personality, although in recent years, there has been a kind of 'revolt' against this way of looking at people and their behaviour. In the 1950s, many drugs came on the market which were used by doctors to alter people's feelings and behaviour. Mental health problems, many of which, I would argue, were rooted in lack of confidence, immediately became even more 'medicalized'. If anyone had a problem with their personality, the important question to be answered was not 'How did this happen?' but, 'I wonder whether this is a case for an anti-depressant or a tranquillizer?' In the 1960s, many people, particularly the young, began to turn to illegal drugs to give them confidence. At the same time, many women turned to their GPs for medication and this created the problem of tranquillizer addiction.

It is not surprising, perhaps, that this method of treating problems became so popular. How much easier it is to think that our anxiety and inability to cope is merely a 'physical disorder'! If this were the case we would be excused automatically from having to engage in the long, and sometimes painful, process of examining ourselves and our lives to look for possible causes. Instead, we can say to ourselves:

Don't feel guilty. After all, having this kind of problem is just like having a broken leg, isn't it? Some people are born lucky aren't they? They have the right genes, the right hormonal balance, the right biochemistry, the right size of brain, and so on, so of course they have more confidence.

Equally, parents can look at their children with a kind of detached interest and say, for example:

She must have inherited a stray gene from somewhere because she is so unlike me. She's always been quiet.

I can see she's got more of her father's blood than her sister has. He's a born worrier, so I know exactly how she's going to turn out.

She's a carbon copy of her mother – her mother always hated making a fuss.

A belief in the theory that personality is determined by our biology neatly lets everyone off the hook!

The world we live in

My own experience, in common with the experience of all the therapists I have known, suggests that self-image is extremely complicated. There *are* some genetic and biological differences between people, but the effect of these differences, especially with regard to confidence, is much less than the effect of parenting and other significant aspects of the world we grew up in.

Understanding our personal history

Here is a list of some of the factors which influence us. Think how each has influenced your self-confidence.

- **Your mother and father**– Did they love you just as you were or did they want you to be something you were not? Did they praise you enough when you did well, or tend merely to criticize you when you didn't? Did they often compare you with others or did they help you assess your achievements in the light of your own potential? Were they good models of confidence themselves? Did they practice what they preached? What was their relationship like? Was it fairly balanced, with two adults confidently asserting their needs and feelings to each other? How did they relate to the rest of the world? Did they perhaps 'hide their lights under bushels', 'put on an act' or were they just themselves?

- **Your position in the family** – Were you an only child, the eldest or the youngest? Were you, for example, given responsibility for looking after younger children? Were you 'babied' or were you treated as 'piggy-in-the-middle' with no special role?

- **Brothers and sisters** – What was their attitude towards you? Were you someone to look up to or were you a threat or someone to be bullied? How successful were they? Were you encouraged to feel competitive with them?

- **Your teachers at school** – Did you feel more confident with some than with others? Were you ever 'teacher's pet'? Were you picked on or taken for granted? How were you disciplined? Was corporal punishment used?

- **Your friends** – Were you bullied, ignored or welcomed into 'the gang'? Did you keep the same friends for a long time or did you have to keep changing them, perhaps because you moved frequently?

- **Your position in society** – Were you from a privileged or underprivileged background? Could you count on receiving the basic necessities of life? Were you discriminated against? Were you expected to do better, or worse than most people?

- **Your lifestyle** – Was it sheltered or were you constantly 'in the limelight' and forced to socialize or compete? Did you experience many changes and upheavals? Did you travel very much?

- **Your religion** – Was it the kind of religion which made you feel good about yourself? Was it full of foreboding or was it optimistic about this life on earth? Did it regard some individuals as more equal than others? Were men given more responsibility, or perhaps privileges, than women?

- **Traumatic events** – Were you physically or emotionally abused at any time? Were you brought up in a peaceful society? Did you lose any important people, jobs or possessions in your life, through no fault of your own?

If we were to continue with this list and consider all the questions it raises, we could easily fill a couple of books! But we only have to reflect on our lives for a few hours to realize just how much we are the products of our upbringing and environment. I have met many hundreds of people suffering with problems of confidence and as yet, I have not met anyone whose problems could not be traced back, to some substantial degree, to their childhood or other important formative experiences. Many people echo the words used by Emily in the film *The Buddy System*. After a lifetime struggling with problems of confidence, she finally confronts her mother (others might confront fathers or teachers), saying:

Maybe if you had given me a chance to be wrong, I would have got some things right. I've spent my whole life afraid of making mistakes.

In contrast, successful, confident women often talk about the positive effect of their upbringing. For example, Shirley Williams acknowledges the influence of her eminent, successful mother, Vera Brittain; Clare Gallagher, who has made her mark in a traditionally male dominated field by becoming manager of the ICI plant in the north of England, said in an interview in the July 1988 issue of *Pages*:

My father and mother treated their sons and daughters as absolute equals. Looking back, I realize that they provided the inspiration I needed.

Sue Lawley, also renowned for making her mark in another male dominated field – the media – speaks of her mother's influence on her ability to combine children and a career successfully in *New Woman* (August, 1988):

But that's how I was brought up. My mother ran a couple of drapery shops. She was a business woman six days a week and also had two children.

Jennifer, a successful money broker, also working in male territory, reckons that the way she was brought up has enabled her to rise to the challenge. As she grew up, she believed that she could do anything. *'There was nothing in my background to suggest that I couldn't.'*

What is the point of looking back?

If we look back we will begin to understand.

Some people may need to take longer than others to find the clues. For example, some parents are sophisticated enough to know the 'right' way to bring children up and this may seem very praiseworthy on the surface. But then children can feel doubly guilty for not being confident and successful.

A guilty conscience is the mother of invention.

Carolyn Wells

Hunting for the double messages, the hidden jealousies, and disguised 'put-downs' may be time-consuming, but it is important because it helps us to accept that our lack of confidence is not an integral part of us – it is a *learned response*. It was learned when we were powerless and were right to feel threatened.

The kind of family we grew up in is perhaps the most important factor of all, Virginia Satir, a world renowned therapist, writes:

I am convinced that there are no genes to carry the feeling of worth. It is learned. And the family is where it is learned . . . an infant coming into the world has no past, no experience in handling himself, no scale on which to judge his own worth. He must rely on the experiences he has with the people around him and the messages they give him about his worth as a person.

We do not need a perfect environment to give us a healthy confidence in ourselves but we do need a 'good-enough' one. D W Winnicott, an excellent and well-known psychoanalyst, wrote:

A good enough environment can be said to be that which facilitates the various individual inherited tendencies . . . it requires a high degree of adaptation to individual infant needs.

Do women have special difficulties?

Yes. In our western society they certainly have. With regard to confidence, these difficulties are, in the main, caused by two major factors:

- Women's subordinate position in society
- Popular attitudes and beliefs about women.

Women in the public world

The feminist movement has, of course, had a tremendous impact on the lives of women. As Lilian Hellman said:

Nobody can argue any longer about the rights of women. It's like arguing about earthquakes.

But, although women have achieved tremendous advances in their battle against sexism and inequality, we still live in a society in which men hold real power over the vast majority of us. Equal opportunity is really still a dream. In Britain, even after being governed for ten years by a female Prime Minister, the nation remains ruled largely by men. Women are slowly creeping up the management ladder in industry and the professional

Women often smile too much when they're nervous

zations, but it will be very many years before any real balance of power in the public world is achieved.

Recent research commissioned by the Equal Opportunities Commission showed that sex discrimination is still widespread and the EOC has called on industry to use negotiation to remove discrimination from working practices.

But sometimes this discrimination takes place even before the women get into the workplace. Sexism manifests itself in many ways, from the career advice given to young girls to the low numbers of women selected for senior posts. A recent report from the Institute of Manpower Studies (published in the *Executive Post*, March, 1988) suggested that personnel chiefs want 'macho' qualities in managers, and as men tend to possess most of these qualities, it is hardly surprising that men occupy the top echelons of power!

Fortunately, women are gathering in force to 'fight' against these difficulties. They are realizing the need to train themselves to become equal competitors with men at work. New organizations such as Women in Enterprise and the National Organization for Women's Management Education (NOWME) have been set up to advance women's training needs and it is interesting, though not surprising, to note that most programmes are likely to include confidence-building courses.

Women in the private world

Although we are all aware of the many changes which have taken place, there is abundant evidence to show that men still hold the real power in most families. This power is often embedded in the family finances.

Current statistics inform us that over 40 per cent of married women now work. But we know that this is often part-time, temporary and low-paid work. Very few wives are able to earn more than their husbands. Working mothers are particularly hard-hit because not only do they have to battle with the general discrimination against women in the world of work, but they also have to cope with many other practical problems.

Even in the most liberal of families, where equality is genuinely being strived for, you find that choices have to be made. The result is that a woman's earning power may be reduced. If one partner's job has to suffer because a child is sick, a child minder is on holiday, or the family decides to move, whose job is protected? Usually it is the man's, if only because it seems to make sound economic sense to protect the job which pays the most and is the most secure. Even as a relatively successful, assertive, professional woman, this is a choice I have had to make many times in my life, and it is a choice that hurts. It can eat away at your self-esteem, especially if you are already lacking in confidence or have other reasons not to feel powerful and in control of your life.

Changes in the way taxes are collected and changes in the way child benefits are distributed are long overdue and, of course, are to be welcomed, but they will not alter the basic reality that, for most women, men will continue to hold the purse strings, and therefore a vast amount of power for very many years to come.

The feminist movement has made us very aware of many other areas in which women have less power than men. It has highlighted, for example, the discrimination that exists in the worlds of education, the arts and sports. We have also been made aware of how power is often abused by men, both physically and emotionally. There is the danger that this abuse could increase as men begin to feel their power being eroded by women. And although, as Gloria Steinhem once said, 'Some of us are becoming the men we wanted to marry,' the vast majority of us remain in a relatively powerless position.

The changing situation for men

Many sociologists and psychologists note that men are in a position of crisis today. Their masculine image of themselves has not only been threatened by the women's liberation movement but by many other changes as well. For example, the nuclear age no longer needs its 'brave soldier'; it's now looking towards the tactful diplomat as its defender, and isn't diplomacy more of a feminine skill?

In the world of big business the aggressive, tough competitor is being replaced by the caring, paternalistic negotiator. Further changes in industry mean that there are fewer jobs in a field in which traditionally men have been able to prove themselves both powerful and macho.

As women, we must remember that, when people feel threatened, they often try to exert more power over others. So, we should prepare ourselves for further resistance from many men to our continuing struggle for true liberation.

In order to counteract such a reaction, and the enormous imbalance of power, a woman must not only excel in her field to gain recognition and just rewards, but she also needs to be physically strong and to sustain immense amounts of confidence in herself and her abilities.

Popular attitudes and beliefs

You only need to watch the advertisements on television, or see children playing 'Mums and Dads' in the school playground to know that the stereotyped attitudes and beliefs about men's and women's roles are alive and well.

Here is a favourite scale used by researchers when looking at these roles. It was compiled by Sandra Bem, after extensive interviews with both men and women from all classes of society in America, who had been asked what they saw as desirable characteristics in men and women (Sandra Bem, 'Measurement

Masculinity and feminity scale	
Masculine items	Feminine items
Aggressive	Affectionate
Ambitious	Cheerful
Analytical	Childlike
Assertive	Compassionate
Athletic	Does not use harsh
Competitive	language
Defends own beliefs	Eager to soothe hurt
Dominant	feelings
Forceful	Easily flattered
Has leadership abilities	Feminine
Independent	Gentle
Individualistic	Gullible
Makes decisions easily	Loves children
Masculine	Loyal
Self-reliant	Sensitive to the needs of
Self-sufficient	others
Strong personality	Shy
Willing to take a stand	Soft-spoken
Willing to take risks	Sympathetic
	Tender
	Understanding
	Warm
	Yielding

Table 1

of Psychological Androgyny', *Journal of Consulting and Clinical Psychology*, 42, 155-162, 1974.)

It is a horrible truth which all therapists are only too aware of, that we tend to grow up with the kind of personality which people expected us to have! You will have noted that the masculine list contains most of the attributes we also associate with confident people. These stereotypes are being fixed constantly in our minds, at both a conscious and unconscious level, through the media, art and even fairy tales.

As 'Daddy's little girls' we grow up dreaming of our prince, who will be bristling with confidence and who will battle through the undergrowth to rescue us. Colette Dowling has called this problem the 'Cinderella Complex' (Colette Dowling, *The Cinderella Complex*, Pocket Books, USA, 1981) and forcibly argues, in her book of the same name, that women must recognize and own this yearning for dependence and wish to be saved.

We must also remember that these stereotypes affect our sexual behaviour as well because not only do we expect the prince to rescue us, but we also expect him to love us. If we look at the list of feminine attributes, we will notice how they may not exactly earn the 'ring of confidence' but they *do* describe the popular fantasy image of the sexy, sensual woman, who always wins the man in the end!

In addition, like Nora in Ibsen's play, *The Doll's House*, we have probably encountered many men who are, in fact, aroused by our very lack of confidence, and we may even have learned to use it as an aphrodisiac! In *The Doll's House*, Helmer says to his wife, Nora:

You have loved me as a wife should love her husband. It was just that you hadn't the experience to realize what you were doing. But do you imagine that you're any less dear to me for not knowing how to act on your own . . .? I shouldn't be a proper man if your feminine helplessness didn't make you twice as attractive to me.

According to one successful woman in industry this kind of seductive behaviour is still commonly observed in the world of business. In an interview by Laura Stonard in *The Sales Professional* in August, 1988, she claimed that women 'use their feminine wiles to get on, wanting all the chivalry and gentler treatment'.

In another world of work – the factory – I recently heard some women talking self-deprecatingly about their work. They said, for example, 'Women can put up with boring jobs; men need something more to occupy them,' and, 'It's not a bad life for a woman anyway.'

Somewhere deep in our unconscious we often associate being 'good' with playing a demure second fiddle to a man. Anita Brookner captures this association in this extract from *A Misalliance* (Grafton, 1987):

Phyllis Duff: a good woman. The picture was now clear. Excellent wife, devoted companion. Keeping up to date, up to scratch, planning her wardrobe – modest but superior with due care but little conceit . . . Mrs Duff had no pretensions to be, nor could she ever be mistaken for, the new breed of woman who takes on the world.

It is not surprising, therefore, that men do, generally, have more confidence if, as women, we perpetuate the stereotypes in our own behaviour and in the way we continue to parent, educate and generally encourage boys and men to possess masculine traits, and girls and women, the feminine ones.

1) LOVING YOURSELF.
2) KNOWING YOURSELF.
3) SKILFUL BEHAVIOUR.
4) OPTIMISM.
5) GENUINENESS.

IN

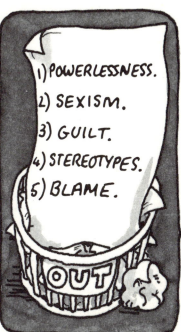

1) POWERLESSNESS.
2) SEXISM.
3) GUILT.
4) STEREOTYPES.
5) BLAME.

OUT

Chapter 2

Changing ourselves and our world

Is change really possible?

Yes, leopards can – and do – change their spots! And the change no longer has to take a life-time. Advances in the fields of psychology and psychotherapy during the past 20 to 30 years have been immense. There are now many alternatives to costly psychoanalytic sessions twice a week for five years. Today, we understand better than ever before how personalities are formed and sustained and we have developed relatively quick methods of enabling people to change their behaviour and feelings, if they wish to do so. The process of changing may not always be easy but it is invariably exciting and challenging, especially if we feel involved and in control of the operation ourselves!

Can we change on our own?

Yes, and even if you do choose to get some help, you will still be doing at least 90 per cent of the work yourself! Self-help is the key to modern methods of helping people to change. That is not to say that professional therapists, like myself, have inadvertently worked ourselves out of a job! It's just that our role and focus have changed. We aim to work in partnership with people. We try not to stand on pedestals, as symbols of perfect mental health. We allow ourselves to be seen as 'real people' with all the failings and imperfections which seem to go hand-in-hand with being human. We do not want to hide our knowledge and skills behind a cloak of mystique; we want to share these and admit our limitations.

Good therapy or counselling is not something that we passively receive and feel grateful for, it is two (or more) people working experimentally, and in partnership, towards a goal which we have set for ourselves, using techniques which we fully understand and have control over.

Another alternative is to join – or create – a self-help group. You can use this book and others, such as those recommended in the suggested Further Reading on page 188, to help you organize yourself.

Whichever method you use you can be sure that the self-help approach will prove to be a confidence booster in itself!

How long will it take?

This will vary from individual to individual. For some people, six months may be all it will take to change some habits and regain their confidence. Others may take several years to reach the stage where they truly believe in their own worth. Until you start the process of change, it is often difficult to predict just how long it will take. I often say that one of the best aspects of my job is that it is never boring; I am constantly being surprised. It seems that the more people I meet and work with, the less inclined I become to make predictions about anyone's potential for change and development – and that includes my own! Each person's problem has an individuality of its own and this is one of the reasons why it is so difficult to produce enough scientific evidence to convince the sceptics that therapy is effective.

How can we begin to change?

I have identified seven essential ingredients for any successful confidence-building programme, and they are as follows:

- **Belief** – We must trust that it is possible to change
- **Motivation** – We must need or want to change
- **Insight** – We must understand ourselves and our behaviour

- **Goals** – We must make sure these are our own and are realistic
- **Practice** – We must spend time and energy rehearsing new behaviours
- **Support** – We must get encouragement
- **Reward** – We must be able to feel the benefit of our hard work.

Let's now consider each of these in some more detail.

Acquiring belief

You could take yourself to the library and look up, in the various psychological and therapeutic journals, research studies on the subject of confidence-building, or it might be more rewarding to listen to, or read about, the personal experiences of other women who have overcome problems. The following is just one example.

My own early childhood

I had the kind of childhood destined to drain the confidence out of any man, woman or beast. Because of my mother's alcoholism, I spent the majority of my childhood years in a series of children's homes. As the eldest of the family, I was a 'big girl' and often felt responsible for the care of my brother and sister. Even as a very young child, I can remember sensing the desperate needs of the family and I tried to work out ways of coping. I quickly learned to assume an air of confidence and optimism which masked my own fears and craving for reassurance.

There were many occasions when my attempts to look after myself and my brother and sister were laughed at by adults. Some of the things which I did must have looked pretty funny to any outsider. For example, when I was about seven, and was alone in the house with my younger brother and baby sister, I attempted to make dinner for my sister, who was screaming with hunger. As I was standing on a chair beside the cooker, boiling some unscrubbed and, presumably, very dirty potatoes, the door was broken open by the police. A social worker came to the kitchen door, burst into laughter when she saw what I was doing, and called the policemen, who also laughed.

Needless to say, my sister was quickly taken from my care and I stood by and silently watched her being placed in a nursery. My brother and I were taken to an even larger, even more impersonal institution, which has no nostalgic happy memories for me.

Our lives continued to be chaotic for very many years to come. Statutory child care, in those days was certainly far from ideal. We were generally bullied and often physically intimidated and abused. The way we were dressed alone indicated to the world that we were second-class citizens. Only occasionally were we taken from this lifestyle to spend some weekends and holidays in the contrasting gentility of my father's middle-class, professional family. We were 'odd-balls' wherever we were, but we learned to be grateful for the small mercies.

The cost to my self-esteem
These experiences gradually eroded my inner confidence, but the world saw an intelligent, capable girl who appeared to be infinitely adaptable and deservingly proud of her 'Good Conduct' badges. My unconscious, however, sent out signals of distress and extreme lack of confidence. I failed the 11-plus exam dramatically, against all expectations, but there had been no school counsellor or psychologist around to interpret these failures.

By the time I was in my teens, my father had remarried and managed, after a long struggle, to get us out of care and give us a taste of a 'normal' family life. But the damage had been done. My mask of confidence and competence had become me. For many years I was even able to kid myself. It was not until my early twenties that the mask began to slip. The first serious depression was treated – very inadequately – by a psychiatrist who arranged an emergency short stay in a mental hospital.

Paying the price
I then embarked on a disastrous lifestyle, which only those people whose self-esteem is rock bottom seem capable of sustaining. Being a woman, this meant that I slid into relationships with men who overpowered me. I used manipulation and guile, so skilfully developed in my childhood, to get back at

the people who hurt me. I chose work (in a helping profession, of course!), to which I was totally unsuited. I failed miserably at it, as a result. In shame, I began to isolate myself socially, spending days and nights locked away on my own.

As my 'outer confidence' disintegrated, so I was faced with the blackness of my inner self, and the predictable happened – I made a pathetic attempt to take my life. This was the turning point for me; I decided that I did want to live and that I did want to change. I was fortunate to be referred for psychotherapy to an amazing woman, to whom I have dedicated this book and who has remained a close friend throughout the rest of my life. She opened up the pathway to my new life.

The road to recovery

It has taken me very many years to reach the point where I can truly describe myself as a 'confident woman' but today I am certainly being rewarded for the struggle. I have a very full life which I thoroughly enjoy. I have family and friends whom I love and who love me. I have work which I find stimulating and satisfying and am confidently planning a future which looks exciting and challenging.

I have told my story because it has given me 'belief'. For many years, I feared to tell the story because I mistakenly thought that people might lose trust in me, as a therapist, if they knew the 'truth' about my background. Of course, I now know that I was wrong and I know that this very personal experience of such problems has given me invaluable knowledge and strength which enables me to give more effective help to others who need to work on their difficulties.

Other women's experiences

Hopefully, not many of you reading this will have experienced such extreme problems, so your road to confidence should be shorter and less bumpy than my own. The vast majority of people with whom I work are able to feel the benefits of confidence-building almost immediately. The following quotes are from some women who have attended courses:

The course has shaken me out of apathy and despair and, at last, I have some energy for me. I am sick of being a martyr.

The fact that I now know that I can handle criticism has transformed my relationships at work.

You'll be pleased to know that when I got back from the course, I applied for three new jobs.

My husband and I are now much closer. He says he prefers the new 'me', and so do I!

I have now left my boyfriend because I now know the kind of relationship I want, I am determined to find it. I've joined a dating agency!

I've stopped letting the kids walk all over me and John even offered to cook the tea on Friday.

At one time all these women, like me, would never have believed such changes were possible in themselves or their lives.

Finding the motivation

Many people think that we have to get to 'rock bottom' before we can really find the motivation to change. That misunderstanding has arisen from observation of 'real life' because that is so often just what *does* happen. Because change feels uncomfortable, we tend to wait until a crisis occurs before we face the need for it. There are several reasons why it doesn't make sense to wait for the crisis, for example:

● The crisis might be overwhelming, leaving you few resources and no energy

● You may never reach crisis point. Many people don't; they jog along in second gear for the whole of their lives leaving a trail of 'if onlys' behind them

● Any behaviour change is effected more swiftly if small steps are taken, when anxiety levels are manageable. The mood of desperation which most crises generate is not conducive to confidence-building.

So, by all means fantasize about the potentially disastrous effect your lack of confidence might have on the pattern of your life . . . but act now!

Acquiring insight

In an earlier chapter, I have already argued the importance of understanding how our particular personality developed, but it is also important that we become acutely aware of our current feelings and our behaviour. This will require:

- A detailed analysis of how you see yourself

- Feedback from people to gain an awareness of how others see you.

I will discuss this further later and there are several exercises in Part 2 which will help you acquire more insight.

Setting realistic goals

People lacking in confidence are experts at setting themselves up for failure. I have already shared my own former skills in this area! Perhaps some of these quotes will ring a few bells!

Only someone as daft as me would have got involved with someone like him.

I knew from the start that this job wasn't for me, but I thought as he suggested it, I'd better give it a try.

Well, I suppose I knew I had it coming to me.

The secret is to aim at getting a balance between 'playing safe' and aiming too high and this is often best achieved by taking small steps first. In this way we have a chance of some success and will get encouragement from the good feeling and rewards which that will bring.

Getting practice

Becoming confident will require you to learn new skills and these, unfortunately, do not come neatly packaged and ready for use. At first our new behaviour will seem strange and unfamiliar to us. For example, becoming confident often requires you to learn a new 'language', a new way of expressing yourself. At the moment I am trying to learn Spanish. Speaking this

language seems very odd and
uncomfortable to me but hopefully
soon I will be able to switch to
'automatic pilot', just as I have done
with French. Until I feel a little more
at ease with the language, I am
choosing to speak to my tape
recorder, in the privacy of my own
home.

There is nothing shameful or 'silly' about practising your new
confident behaviour in the bath, or in front of a mirror. If you
have access to audio-visual equipment you may find rehearsing
in front of the camera good practice. Alternatively, you could
try role-playing with the help of a sympathetic friend, self-help
group or counsellor.

Finding support

There is nothing like working
through a confidence-building
programme to find out who your
true friends are! You have to find
friends who want you to change and
will encourage and support you.

Remember that if people 'like you the way that you are' they
must be getting some reward for themselves through your lack
of confidence. Maybe you make them feel more powerful,
maybe they stand a better chance of promotion, maybe they
do not have to bother to change their behaviour if you are not
complaining – or maybe they just get a 'kick' out of abusing
you! You could have been told that your new behaviour is bossy,
selfish, or unfeminine. If you judge that it is not, and want to
continue, you may have to choose new friends.

Reaping the rewards

Learning theory has taught us that we acquire new skills faster
and more efficiently if we are rewarded when we achieve, rather
than punished when we do not. Most unconfident people will
have experienced their fair share of punishment, both from
others and from themselves. Getting rewards will be a relatively
new experience.

In the early stages of learning a new skill, we may not get sufficient rewards from the 'outside world' to allay our anxieties. So, we must learn to reward ourselves. This may mean treating yourself to a special night out or a present if you have tried to do something which you

know was very risky for you, even though to others the action may have seemed very ordinary. For example, you may have set yourself the task of striking up three conversations at a party. The people who are with you may not appreciate your achievement, and so will not think to say 'Well done'.

Equally we may not get immediate rewards because the task which we have chosen to use our new-found skills on may be very complex and long-term. You may be very tempted to give up when you hear people say: 'Don't bother; it's not worth it. Life's too short. It's best to keep the peace.'

1) BELIEF
2) SELF-HELP
3) PRACTICE
4) SUPPORT
5) REWARDS

IN

1) CYNICISM
2) MYSTIQUE
3) FANTASY
4) FEAR
5) MARTYRDOM

OUT

As you become more confident, your life will begin to change and become more exciting and satisfying. Then there will be no shortage of rewards!

Chapter 3
Self-knowledge

Many famous and successful people have mastered the outward skills of confident behaviour and their very success is a credit to this achievement. However, sometimes they disclose in their autobiographies, or revealing interviews, that they feel very different inwardly. My daughter recently attended a concert given by the pop singer Michael Jackson, and while she was there, my husband showed me an article in a magazine he was reading. It quoted Michael Jackson as saying, 'I think I'm the world's loneliest man.' Inwardly, he still feels just as he did when he was at school 'when there was one girl I liked but I wasn't able to tell her. I was too embarrassed.'

Cilla Black, another very popular and outwardly confident figure, said, in a similarly revealing interview in the *TV Times*, 3 September, 1988: 'I hate walking into a crowded room . . . When I'm out with friends it won't be me that is the life and soul of the party.' She, too, recalls fears from her childhood: 'I'll never forget my first day at school. One of my plaits came undone and I burst into tears. I was afraid to ask the teacher if she would do it for me.'

Many famous women would echo the well-known agony aunt and author, Claire Rayner, when she revealed, very courageously, in a recent radio interview: 'I would like to be the person that people clearly think I am.' Although Claire Rayner maintains that this discrepancy between her 'public' persona and her 'private' persona does not cause her great concern, many others find the strain of 'living up to appearances' intolerable. Marilyn Monroe's tragic story is an obvious example.

Another film star, Elizabeth Taylor, vividly describes difficulties, in her recent book, *Elizabeth Takes Off*. Her first step towards recovery, she explained in an interview by Claire Rayner for BBC Radio Four, was to break down old fears, doubts and anxieties. After a considerable amount of soul-searching and personal development work, she proudly claimed that: '. . . now my exterior and interior are in harmony, I really feel as good as I look. And dammit, I know I look good!' (Elizabeth Taylor, *Elizabeth Takes Off*, Macmillan, 1988).

We may not all be able to look like Elizabeth Taylor, or indeed want to look like her, but these next two chapters are going to concentrate on ways in which you too can build up your inner confidence so that you can also feel as good as you look – or intend to look – when you have mastered the skills of confidence!

The two essential keys to feeling good inwardly are:

- **Self-knowledge**

and

- **Self-love**

In my experience, women who lack confidence rarely demonstrate mastery in either of these two areas. More often than not they are confused about their very identity and they lead the kinds of lives which would indicate that they give their own needs very low priority.

In Section Four of this book, there are many exercises which are designed to help you develop in both of these areas, but let's first have a more detailed look at each area in turn.

Why knowing yourself is important

If you have a tendency to feel that time spent working in this area would be 'self-indulgent', just think of the following advantages we stand to gain if we become fully acquainted with ourselves and our potential:

- **We feel more in control** – We are able to relax and are less prone to getting unpleasant shocks about ourselves, for example, 'Oh, I surprised myself. I didn't think I could be so nasty (or frightened, or weak).'

- **We can use our time effectively** – For example, we can choose to spend more time doing things we are good at, or learn to improve those areas which we are weakest in, we can set realistic goals for ourselves

- **We can protect ourselves** – If we acknowledge that we have a particular weakness, we can make allowances for this and we will be better able to defend ourselves from both fair and unfair criticism.

Let's consider some of the common arguments people tend to use to convince themselves that they do not wish to acquire more self-knowledge, for example: 'I am afraid that when I start delving, I will get some unpleasant surprises and I will end up not liking myself.'

This is a very understandable fear because confidence is so highly valued in our society. Consequently, those who lack it may well have doubts about their own self-worth. These are likely to have been fostered and reinforced by important people in their lives who may have been, or may still be, treating them as 'lesser mortals'. My experience is that embarking on a voyage

I am afraid when I start delving, I will get some unpleasant surprises . . .

of self-discovery is highly rewarding for these people, and full of very pleasant surprises. Strengths and virtues may have been obliterated previously by doubt and anxiety. For people lacking in confidence, the process of getting to know yourself better usually means uncovering and reclaiming parts of yourself which you truly admire and value. For many people I have known, this has meant finding their buried creativity and sensuality, for example.

'Oh no, I wouldn't know where to start . . . It's too complex, and anyway, I'm always changing.'

People who make this kind of excuse are often admitting that their real fear is that introspection will send them mad. The reason for this fear is that they often actually feel a little 'mad', that is, not in control of their feelings and behaviour. They cannot, for example, understand why they suddenly 'dried up' in the middle of a speech or an interview, or why they should have felt intimidated by someone they considered their match. In fact, having 'insight' (to use the more technical name for self-awareness), would, in most psychiatrists' eyes, be a contra-indication of madness. The more self-knowledge we have, the more control we can exert over our feelings and behaviour.

There's no point in finding out who I am, or what I want, because you can't control other people, or change what fate has in store for you.

Of course, other people's behaviour and events can have considerable impact on us and our lives, but we need to feel that we have some control over the way we are being influenced. Confident people are continually adapting and changing, according to the different situations and relationships they are experiencing, but they do not lose a sense of their own 'core identity'. They do not feel overwhelmed or supremely anxious, because they feel in charge of this changing process. People who lack confidence, on the other hand, either tend to stick rigidly to one persona or use markedly different faces for every situation, so you are often not quite sure who you are going to meet! They know that the faces which they use are often inappropriate for certain situations, but they feel unable to control their behaviour.

Feeling powerless is central to problems of confidence. People who feel this way have almost certainly been abused by someone or by some people who took advantage of them when they *were* actually powerless. The most effective way that I know of, of changing this kind of thinking, is to identify the culprits, as we began to do in the last chapter (see pages 20-21).

Discovering your identity

So, assuming that you are now convinced of the value of gaining more self-knowledge, it will be helpful to start by asking yourself the following questions:

What kind of person am I?

One of the most difficult aspects of my job is that I am often asked to do references for people. Summing up someone's personality, aptitudes and skills, usually on one sheet of paper, is an awesome task, but I imagine that most of us would experience even greater difficulty if we were asked to do a similar exercise on ourselves! You can put yourself to the test by completing Exercises 10-12 on pages 136-8 in Section four.

Most people, when asked to describe themselves, begin to talk about the 'roles' they have in life, for example, a teacher; a mother of two boys; a tennis player; a housewife. So, if you also feel comfortable starting from this point, begin to list your behaviour, feelings and thoughts in each role that you 'play'. Just jot down what comes into your head, without thinking too hard, at first. You can always add to it later. For example, my own might look like this:

My role as 'Mother'

- **My behaviour** – Looking after; encouraging; teaching; listening; learning; cooking; homemaking

- **My feelings** – warm; loving; protective; frustrated; angry; happy; excited; puzzled; satisfied

- **My thoughts** – Wondering how other mothers do it; judging rights and wrongs; planning the future; remembering nostalgic memories of the past; comparing my childhood to that of my children; wondering if I am being too protective

My role as therapist

● **My behaviour** – Listening; encouraging; teaching; giving information; leading; following; confronting

● **My feelings** – Caring; warm; excited; interested; satisfied; relieved; frustrated

● **My thoughts** – planning; looking at different possibilities; comparing; wondering if I am being effective

Completing this kind of exercise can help us build up a very realistic picture of the kind of person we are. We find that certain 'themes' keep cropping up (for instance, my own caring behaviour; my habit of comparing myself), or that we seem to be experiencing a particular feeling in most of our roles (for example, my excitement and frustration).

We can often learn even more by comparing one role with another and noting which, perhaps, gives us the opportunity to exercise a less commonly used side of ourselves, or which gives us the most scope for relaxing and just 'being ourselves'.

What are my strengths and weaknesses?

Confident people are aware of both their good points and their bad points and feel comfortable about other people knowing these, too. I have found that the people attending my courses can much more easily share the latter than the former!

Unfortunately, for many people, it still seems socially unacceptable to share their strengths openly with each other. For example, even in this competitive age, when you look through most job applications, you notice a marked tendency for people – especially women – to 'play safe' by underselling themselves. This tendency can also be noted in the personal columns of papers where people advertise hoping to find friends and partners. Here, humour is very often used as a cover for the embarrassment of declaring your virtues openly to the world.

People lacking in confidence have usually had an extra-strong dose of 'hide-your-light-under-a-bushel' messages programmed into them and they often need an extra-strong antidote to counteract that! The boasting exercises on pages 138 and 148 are most effective and a good boost for anyone who feels their self-esteem needs the occasional 'recharge'. And don't worry, I have never known anyone 'overdose' on them yet, or, indeed, become permanently addicted! Practise them until you can openly relate your strengths in a relaxed manner, using a strong, clear voice without becoming giggly or crippled by other awkward behaviours.

Similarly, practise the exercises on pages 137-8, which will help you to assertively own your faults and weaknesses. They will help you to be more accepting and forgiving of yourself. I have found that most people lacking in confidence have impossible expectations of themselves. They often demand nothing less than perfection from themselves and are consumed with guilt for not living up to these exacting standards. Interestingly, they also have a tendency to expect these standards from people they have designated as their 'models' of confidence. As someone who frequently finds herself in this position, I would like to say that it is very tiring, standing up on that pedestal unless, of course, you really are made of stone!

In addition, these exercises will provide a very good foundation from which to practise the assertive techniques for coping with criticism. I will discuss this in the next chapter.

What are my values?

They call him 'Jigsaw' because every time he's faced with a problem he goes to pieces.

Anon

Perhaps one of the greatest telltale signs of lack of inner confidence is a persistent difficulty in making decisions. Sometimes this difficulty is very explicitly portrayed through typically anxious and procrastinating behaviour, but it can also take the opposite form. Often people will make decisions too quickly, because they are keen to take the familiar, safe road, which means they have, in effect, avoided making any real decision.

Whatever the 'symptom', the cause of persistent difficulties in making decisions, almost certainly has something to do with the person not being very sure about their values.

In order to feel strong in ourselves, we need to have our own personal set of 'commandments' or 'rules' according to which we generally lead our lives. We may choose to review and adapt these constantly as we change and our lives change, but we should always be aware of the basic framework within which we are operating.

When people first start to do personal development work, they are often shocked when they become aware of how muddled their own philosophy of life is. They realize that they have unconsciously taken on board a hotchpotch of values from their mothers, fathers, teachers, church leaders, politicans, bosses, husbands, friends and other significant people in their lives. Often these values are at war with one another. We have all experienced, to a greater or lesser degree, the debilitating effects of this kind of interminable inner battle:

I don't think I should really say anything to him but I know that I ought to . . . Perhaps, if I did, he would think I was stupid, but if I didn't, she would think I was silly. Maybe I should just do what Mary suggests, but on the other hand Joan never does it that way. It says in this book that we ought always to be like this but it says in this other one that we ought to be like that . . .

When we find ourselves persistently thinking like this, we are being controlled by *fear* – a fear which is almost certainly rooted in a deep-seated terror of rejection. The price which we know that we often have to pay for having a clear value system of our own is that *some* people may not like our ideas and behaviour and may not want to be with us – that's the reality. The frightening fantasy is that *no one* will want to know us!

> If we want to feel truly confident, we must break the habit of trying to please all people, all of the time!

I have purposely used the word 'habit' because it is important to remember that this behaviour is *learned* behaviour and therefore it can be *unlearned*. It was probably learned in childhood, at an age when we were too young to risk rejection, a time when we really needed the rewards we earned through being 'nice little girls'.

Many successful women are also still trying to please their mothers and not themselves. A woman who was a recent runner-up in the Business Woman of the Year competition tells this revealing story from *Pages* (August, 1988):

An article in a national newspaper mentioned that my evening meal for the family normally consisted of a prepared take-away. My mum rang me up and threatened to write to the paper, she was so annoyed with the idea that I didn't cook a full meal. I reassured her that the article had given a misleading impression.

Outdated values about being a housewife are some of the hardest to budge. Many of us still share the sentiments expressed in this quote from Erma Brombeck:

No one knows what their life expectancy is, but I have a horror of leaving this world and not having anyone in the entire family know how to replace a toilet tissue spindle.

Fortunately the world at large seems to be able to contain an infinite number of people with differing philosophies, but often those who lack confidence have lived a 'sheltered' life and their personal world may be very small and limited in its potential. Once we feel secure and confident about our own values, we are in a stronger position to expand our horizons. We will begin to look for – and find – people who are less likely to reject us, people who either share our own values or who are secure enough in themselves to be able to respect differences in others.

Understanding your personality

If you have worked your way through the previous questions and completed the appropriate exercises in Section 4, you will probably have built up quite a complex picture of yourself. Now is the time to attempt to consolidate this knowledge, so that you can see the 'wood', as well as the 'trees'. You can judge whether some areas may be overgrown and out of control, whether the young saplings have enough space and nourishment, whether some species can harmoniously co-exist with others, or whether for the sake of the 'whole' you may need to ruthlessly uproot the diseased and the discordant. You will then be in a better position to judge whether this is a suitable job for a lone 'do-it-yourself' forester, or whether you may need to recruit some extra hands, or professional expertise from time-to-time.

When we are embarking on the analysis of any problem it often helps to work within a framework. There are now many different psychological 'frameworks' available for us to use. One that I, and many other people, have found useful is Transactional Analysis or TA.

TA is a theory which was developed by an American psycho-analyst called Eric Berne. It has achieved popularity because it was relatively simple and used everyday language instead of the more technical and complex language which began to predominate as psychology grew in scientific status. In my suggested reading list on page 188, I have included several books which I would recommend that you read if you are interested in exploring this model further, and in Section four I have included several TA exercises which I have found very useful. Most people say that the theory starts to come alive only when you start applying it to your own personality and life through exercises, so don't be tempted to skip the practical work!

In the meantime, I will briefly summarize the parts of the theory which are particularly relevant to confidence-building.

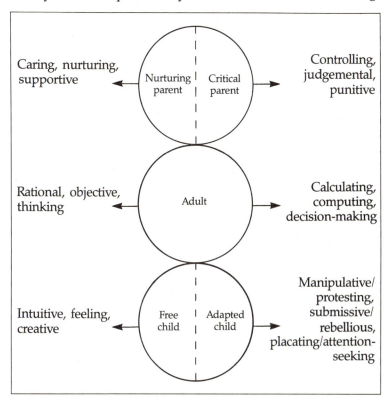

Transactional analysis

Just as in Freudian analysis, TA suggests that the personality has three fairly distinct parts, which Berne named the **Parent**, **Adult** and **Child**. These different parts of our personality are called **Ego states**, that is, they are a set of feelings which affect our behaviour. As the theory has developed these parts have become subdivided, and the most commonly used of these are **Critical parent**, **Nurturing parent**, **Free child** and **Adapted child**. This diagram is used to illustrate the basic theory:

Table 2 is designed to help you identify these ego states in your own and other people's personalities by observing the stereotypical signs in behaviour.

Here are some important points to remember about ego states:

● The feelings which govern them are rooted in our childhood experiences. We have been 'programmed' automatically to behave in certain ways when we re-experience feelings from our childhood in our adult life. However, sometimes we are not consciously aware of these feelings.

● We move in and out of these states but at any one point in time one state will tend to play 'top dog' and exert the most influence on our behaviour

● In order to communicate well with other people, we need to be in an ego state which complements and does not 'jar' with the ego state of the other person. (See Tables 3 and 4 on pages 52-4.)

● Certain ego states are more appropriate than others for particular situations. For example, the Adult state is appropriate for making rational decisions, such as which political party you should vote for; which educational course is most suitable for you, and so on; and the Free child state is appropriate for having fun, such as at parties; in bed with your lover.

People who lack confidence often experience the following problems with regard to their ego states:

	Critical Parent	Nurturing Parent	Adult	Free Child	Adapted Child
Words and phrases	'should', 'ought', 'do', 'don't', 'must', 'never', 'always', 'good', 'bad', demand, punish, critical, insist, 'you can't', 'don't tell me', 'if I were you', 'don't ask, do it', 'why don't you', 'there's no need'	care, support, help, protect, teach, aid, educate, heed, watch, poor thing, there-there, let me help you, don't be worried, I'll get it for you, You'll be fine, I'll protect you, relax, it's Okay	how, when, where, why, who, probability, facts, compute, test, data, calculate, decide, alternative, result, objective, problem-solve, statistics, options, I see your point, I understand, I recognise	fun, wow, joy, magic, creative, fantasy, intuitive, scared, love, hate, natural, spontaneous, I wish, I want, Oh boy!, Ouch!, Ughhh!, laugh	please, sorry, rebel, adapt, obey, comply, yes sir, no sir, thank you, I should, I must, I had better, manipulative, did I do alright?, I can't, I'll try, if only, it's not my fault, one of these days
Gestures and postures	finger pointing, pounding the table, hands on hips, frowning, scowling, rolling eyes upwards in disgust, furrowed brow, head leaning back or straining forward, looking down over rim of glasses	pat on the back, open arms, smiling, holding, consoling, touching, nodding, sympathetic or proud eyes, loving, encouraging	level eye contact, straight (not stiff) posture, slightly tilted head, confident appearance, alert, open, thoughtful, appearance of active listening	uninhibited, free, spontaneous, loose, joyful or exhilarated posture, bright eyed, exaggerated motions	pouting, sad, helpless, slumped shoulders, dejected, downcast or upcast eyes, sulky, head tilted to one side, forlorn appearance
Tones of voice	judgemental, stern, harsh, condescending, sneering, punitive, indignant, commanding	sympathetic, caring, concerned, loving, supportive, soothing, soft, comforting	clear, confident, calm, even, relaxed, enquiring, self-assertive	belly laughing, loud, noisy, free, excited, giggling, energetic, chuckling	appealing, nagging, complaining, placating, whining, mumbling, grumbling, protesting, asking permission, submissive

Table 2

Complementary Parallel Transactions

These are transactions which take place when the person who is responding is in the ego-state which the speaker is actually addressing and therefore she/he responds in a way which is 'in tune' with the speaker's statement or question — both feel they are on the same wave-length.

Examples	
S — 'I think the government should reduce taxation for the low-paid and start doing it's job properly, don't you?' R — 'Yes, it's about time that they showed they really care about people.'	
S — 'I am interested in doing a teacher training course and I am trying to decide which one to do.' R — 'I suppose it would depend on whether it is important to you to find one with a good Art department. I've heard that the one in Manchester has a good reputation.'	
S — 'This party is really boring.' R — 'Isn't it just! Let's start some dancing.'	

S — 'I'm fed-up with housework, I feel like going on strike!' R — 'If you stopped moaning and started working, you wouldn't feel depressed.'	
S — 'Please will you hurry up and get that report here, I haven't got all day.' R — 'I'm sorry, silly me, I was day dreaming. I'll do it straight away.'	

Table 3

Crossed Transactions

These are transactions which take place when the person who is responding is in a different ego-state to that which the speaker is actually addressing. The two people will not therefore be operating on the same wave-length and will get their wires crossed.

Examples	
S — 'Can you tell me the price please?' R — 'Can't you see for yourself, it's written on the back!'	

S — 'Wow! You look really gorgeous tonight, let's have a cuddle.' R — 'It's late and I have to get up at six tomorrow morning.'	
S — 'You seem tired and overworked, I think you should have the week-end off.' R — 'I am not as tired as I was last week, and if this project is not completed by Monday, I will not get paid.'	
S — 'I'm feeling really nervous about it, what do you think would be the best thing to do?' R — 'Oh, dear if you're feeling that bad let me do it for you?'	

Table 4

- Their ability to function well in their Adult state may be seriously impaired. They will tend to operate too frequently in their Adapted child state (that is, they will be over-concerned about the impact of their behaviour on others). This is probably because they were heavily influenced in their childhood, by adults who, in their turn, operated too frequently in their Parent states. They therefore never gave their children a chance to develop a confidence in their own ability to make decisions.

For example, are you still locked emotionally in a bond with any, or all, of your parent figures? Are you still trying to please them, or alternatively, annoy them? Do you clean the house rapidly when you hear they are coming to stay? Do you long for them to be as excited as you are by a new job or a boyfriend? Or, are you staying married to someone just because your mother told you he was wrong for you? Do you purposely wear certain clothes when you see your father, just as a statement. If this kind of behaviour rings bells for you, you are not alone; I hear many similar stories every week.

- They often confuse their Adult messages with their Parent messages. The TA term for this confusion is 'contamination'.

  For example, have you ever made what you thought, at the time, was a rational decision (choosing a job, a course or an outfit to wear), but on reflection realized that you were really doing what you thought you *ought* to do, and not what was really in your best interests? Perhaps you have been shopping at the sales and have had this kind of experience. You see a dress which you like and which you know will be ideal for work. Your true Adult has worked out that you could well afford to buy the dress and the price is very reasonable. But, your Critical parent slips in (cleverly disguised as Adult logic), and convinces you that the purchase would be extravagant. ('Didn't Mum always say that you only ever needed three good outfits for work. You can always dress them up.') You go home, sleep on it and realize that you were mad not to buy the dress. You return to the shop, only to find that it has been sold!

  Of course, we can all live without the odd dress but perhaps you may recall this kind of 'contamination' affecting some more major decisions in your life.

- There are frequent internal battles between the ego states for 'top dog' position. For example, do you find yourself getting too emotional when you are trying to be sensible and logical? Or do you find yourself being a kill-joy when everyone is trying to let their hair down, or, alternatively, playing the clown when others are trying to speak seriously to you? Do you find a bossy tone creeping into your voice when you are trying to teach someone a skill? Do you say 'sorry' when you know that it really wasn't your fault?

● They often find themselves in an inappropriate ego state for the occasion. For example, do you often 'get your wires crossed' with other people? Do you have the feeling that you're not speaking the same language? Does your behaviour often feel awkward? Do other people feel embarrassed by your behaviour?

● They often, perhaps unknowingly, disguise their behaviour by appearing to act in one ego state when they are in fact operating from another. (When two or more people do this following a regular and predictable pattern it is called a 'game'.) For example, do you ever play 'little girl' in order to get someone to do something which you think they ought to do? Do you ever pretend to agree with someone or appear to be listening attentively just in order to please them? Do you do things for other people in the guise of helping them, when really you are doing it because you have dismissed the alternatives, or are wanting to please?

TA can also help us understand our general philosophy of life, as well as these more specific behaviours and feelings. It suggests, in common with most other psychological theories, that our basic emotional attitude towards ourself, others and life in general is set out in the early years of our childhood. Thomas Harris, in his bestselling book *I'm OK – You're OK* (Pan, 1970) introduces four typical, basic 'philosophies' which children adopt as a result of their early experiences and which tend to affect their behaviour throughout their adult life. He calls them **life positions** and they can be summarized as follows:

● **I'm not OK; you're OK** – This is a natural position for newborn, helpless babies who are totally dependent on adults. They can only passively wait to be 'told' by them, through their caring actions, whether or not they are valuable and worthy. The basic attitude to life is: 'My life is not worth much; I'm nothing compared to you.'

● **I'm not OK; you're not OK** – This is the position which children get into when they have been neglected, unloved or abused by the adults responsible for them. They were unable to find a way of protecting themselves and feel that there is no hope. Their basic attitude to life is that life is not worth anything at all; we might as well all be dead. So, it doesn't matter what we do or who we hurt

- **I'm OK; you're not OK** – This position is a result of the child finding a way of emotionally defending herself, or himself, from the hurt experienced at the hands of adults. Often this hurt is of an extreme nature and the child gets a sense of self-worth from just being a survivor – a 'tough cookie' who is always armed for expected combat. The basic attitude to life is: 'I'm going to get what I can, though I'm not expecting too much. Your life is not worth much; you are dispensable. Get out of my way.'

- **I'm OK; you're OK** – As children grow up, if they have received 'good-enough' parenting, they begin to be able to use their Adult ego state to enable them to make a conscious decision to *choose* this fourth position. They are able to move from one of the other three more infantile positions because they can now weigh up all the evidence logically and objectively which they have accumulated from their total life experience. The basic attitude to life is: 'Life is worth living; let's live it to the full.'

An important point to remember is that when any of us is feeling very anxious, threatened or powerless, we have a tendency to slip back into one of the first three more infantile positions and adopt these basic attitudes. Which one we choose will depend on our particular childhood experiences. For the vast majority of women who lack confidence, the familiar position is number one: 'It's my fault, not theirs.' Women usually get depressed rather than angry.

In addition, as we have already noted, the Adult part of the personality is often less well developed in people who lack confidence, so their ability to take up the more 'logical' fourth position is understandably impaired. Furthermore, when we considered the stereotyped attitudes to the two sexes we noted that women, in our society, are expected, and encouraged to be less logical (Adult) and more emotional (Child)!

Scripts

To further explain how our childhood messages affect our adult life, Berne suggests that we all live by an unconscious 'script'. It is as though someone has pre-written the play of our life and that if you can read the script you will know what the ending is likely to be. The 'playwrights' may include your parents or any other individual or group which has had a strong influence on you. The script is an amalgam of messages which have set your unconscious expectation of life and which, in turn, influence the kind of decisions you make about jobs, relationships, health priorities etc. They will help determine whether you become a 'winner' or 'loser' in life. Here are some examples based on some generally accepted stereotypes.

Examples of cultural scripts

- **British** – We are stable; we are important; look at our history; we won the war; one should never get over-emotional; good breeding counts for more than money; cold showers are good for you

- **American** – We are pioneers; individuals need to compete and work hard to survive; it's good to take risks even if they may shorten your life; we are always on the move; our lives will always change

- **Jewish** – We are victims; people will always try to persecute us; we are special; God has a plan; only trust your own kind; blood is thicker than water; education is power; we are cultured; father knows best.

Examples of family scripts

- We Browns have always been farmers; we Turners always have big families; you're just like your mother, and she always had a temper; no one in our family has ever made it to university, we're not cut out for it; we've always been strong Tories; we can only afford to send one of you to a public school, and I know you'll understand that education is more important for boys; you're Daddy's girl; it never pays to be pushy; you were always a difficult child.

Many children nowadays are openly questioning the 'scripts' written for them by their parents. I see evidence of this just from reading the problem pages of my daughters' magazines. The following letter is one example:

I haven't had a boyfriend for at least five years. I know this may sound stupid but my dad has said that the eldest girl in our family never gets married. His aunty and his sister were the eldest and they never got married at all. I'm frightened about this because I so much want to settle down with a family of my own one day

As with many children who are unhappy, I looked outside my home for my sense of values. My naive Roman Catholic faith seemed to provide all the answers; it explained why I was suffering on this earth and gave me some hope for a different future – even if it did mean that I had to die before I would find it! I chose a particular saint to be named after and, looking back on my life, I am amazed at the influence the story of this saint has had on my behaviour and attitudes. For years, I know that I, unconsciously, acted out Saint Elizabeth's script, meekly and rather ineffectually defending 'the poor' against 'the tyrant'.

But we need not bow to this kind of predetermination. Once

we understand how we have become the kind of person we are, and why we are leading our life down the loser's road, we can make plans to change. We can take power into our own hands and start doing the necessary repair work. For most women, this will mean starting at the root of the problem, that is, moving from **I'm not OK; you're OK** to **I'm OK; you're OK**. We can do this by:

- **Improving our self-esteem** – by learning to love and like ourselves and lead our lives accordingly. (See Chapter 4.)

- **Developing our Adult** – by taking a rational, logical problem-solving approach to changing our behaviour so that we can, as adults, learn the behavioural skills associated with confidence which our childhood, and our culture, have failed to give us. (See Chapters 5 to 9.)

Chapter 4

Improving your self-esteem

Actions, generally, speak louder than words. You must prove to yourself that you really do matter. At first, you may have to go a little 'overboard', and you may need to reassure yourself and, perhaps, the people you live with, that you are not going to drown in a sea of self-love. Start in small ways so that you feel you are in control of the ship!

Change the way you talk about yourself

- Stop putting yourself down. Ask friends to remind you when you use phrases such as: 'It's only me'; 'This is probably just another of my silly ideas but . . .'; 'Well, I'll try, but I may not be very good at it'; 'I'm such an idiot! I'm sure it must have been . . .'; 'I don't mind . . .'; 'I could kick myself . . .'; or 'I'm hopeless at . . .'

- Use 'I' to ask for what you need and want. Replace statements such as: 'Do you think I could possibly have . . .'; 'Would you mind very much if I . . .?'; 'One gets very . . .'; or 'People shouldn't . . .'
  with statements like: 'I want . . .'; 'I would like . . .'; 'I need . . .'; or 'Can I . . .?'

Start to reward yourself

First, make a list of special treats for yourself. You may find this more difficult than it sounds. Most unconfident women do. This is because your childhood and your subsequent life will have been quite barren of treats. Start with small pleasures which you could give yourself and work towards identifying the very special ones. My abbreviated list reads something like this:

Freshly brewed pot of Earl Grey tea

A walk on the moor

An hour in the bath with a novel

Watching a soap opera on TV with my family

Tea at one of my favourite cafés

Stilton cheese

A new book or record

A meal out with friends

A Turkish bath

A weekend in the country

A holiday abroad

Having my bedroom redecorated.

The next step is to start giving yourself these treats on these kinds of occasions.

- When you have attempted to do something which was difficult or frightening

- When you have succeeded in achieving a goal

- When someone has been nasty to you

- When you have had some bad news

- When you are feeling blue

- When you are not well

- Just before you are about to do something very nerve-racking, for example, going for an interview or an exam, or even going to a party.

Look after your body

Nurturing and caring for your body is one of the most fundamental ways in which you can convince yourself of your value as a person. Recent medical research has now scientifically proved a truth, which inherited wisdom has always tried to impress upon us, that the health of mind and the body are inextricably linked. I know that I have had to learn my lesson the hard way. Like so many people I know, I had to become seriously ill before I fully acknowledged the importance of this relationship. A number of years ago, in response to emotional problems which I was experiencing, I developed serious arthritic symptoms and chronic sinusitis. Now that I have changed myself and my life, the former symptoms have completely disappeared and the latter only emerge when I allow myself to get over-stressed.

Leading a confident lifestyle requires energy. We need to be physically fit to have access to all our potential energy. I know that there are many illnesses and disabilities which we cannot do much to prevent, but we can, at least, try to avoid them. The majority of people I work with admit that they have 'let their body go'.

> Not caring about your body is one of the biggest 'put-downs' you can possibly give to yourself

Traditionally, women have not spent as much time as men on keeping fit. Sport, for example, is still predominantly a male pastime. If you look at the advertisements trying to attract women to health clubs, sports centres or exercise clubs the emphasis is nearly always on the fact that the activity will make them look good. Yes, confident women want to look good, but it is even more important to feel good!

So, check your patterns in relation to:

- **Diet** – Check the nutritional value of your diet and take supplements if you know you are going to be under any physical or mental stress. Cut out, or cut down on, harmful foods, drinks and additives

- **Sleep** – I know that I get more edgy and nervous when I am tired. Are you getting enough sleep for you?

- **Exercise** – You don't have to be a sports fanatic, but just check that you have adequate exercise

- **Stress** – Learn to recognize the signs in your own body which indicate you are under too much stress. For me, they include catarrh, backache, flab and spots! Find ways of preventing or alleviating the stress, such as meditation, massage or simply long, hot baths.

Respect your feelings

They rarely lie. If you are hiding your feelings from yourself, or from anyone else, you are hiding you!

Watch out for the bodily sensations which can give you clues to the emotions you are experiencing. These are often in evidence long before our minds are ready – or willing – to give us the message. Sometimes the signs are to be found in very small movements or sensations, particularly if we are feeling an emotion which an old 'message' tells us ought to be censored. For example, if you find yourself inexplicably tapping your finger, exaggerate the movement and you may find your anger or frustration!

Find *appropriate* ways of expressing your feelings. Pent up emotions drain our energy and are a major factor in contributing to many of the physical and emotional problems which those lacking in confidence tend to suffer. Such complaints may include: migraine: backache; stomach and bowel disorders; phobias; obsessions; depression.

Feelings *need* physical expression, so give yourself the permission you may never have had in your childhood to express them fully. Don't listen to the old injunctions such as: 'Don't be a cry baby'; 'Don't raise your voice to me'; 'Stop grinning like a Cheshire cat'; 'Don't giggle'; 'Pull yourself together'; and 'Be brave'. If you are sad, cry; if you are angry, shout and stamp; if you are nervous, shudder and shake; if you are happy, have a good laugh or scream for joy!

If that feels like too tall an order (and it would be for very many people), begin by acknowledging the existence of your feelings, at least verbally. You do get some relief from simply saying: 'I'm nervous'; 'I'm feeling sad'; or 'I'm frustrated'.

Beware of including a put-down. Stop yourself from prefixing a statement about your feelings with: 'I know it's silly but . . .'; 'I'm sorry but . . .'; 'It's really childish of me but . . .'; or 'I know I ought to be able to control it but . . .'

Make sure your body gives a compatible message. For example, don't smile when you declare your anger, or frown when you acknowledge your pleasure.

Alter your lifestyle

Check whether or not you are leading the right life for you. Some of the exercises mentioned in Section four will help you to do this. Make changes which will ensure, for example, that:

- You can live according to your values, as far as possible

- You have the right balance between work and play for you

- You have the kind of relationships which you want

- You have scope to change and develop

Look your best

Most people change their appearance in some way after doing a confidence-building course. It may be a small change, such as a new hairstyle or different make-up, or it may be a stunning transformation, such as a completely different style of dressing.

You may well have adopted, either consciously or unconsciously, an appearance designed to please others or you may still have an unwanted 'message' ringing in your ears which says appearance isn't importnat, or that a concern for it reflects vanity and selfishness. You may have had the same kind of mother as a little girl that I saw recently when I was shopping with my daughter for her school uniform. This little 10-year-old girl obviously needed a new school skirt and my daughter and I watched, open-mouthed, as the assistant and the mother discussed the pros and cons of the various options. Eventually a sale bargain, at least two sizes too big, was chosen, presumably for reasons of economy, although the mother's diamond would have suggested economy was not necessary. Throughout the transaction, the girl's opinion was neither asked for, nor proffered. At one stage, the assistant, perhaps moved, as we were, by the sad little eyes, tentatively suggested the skirt was a little too long. The mother retorted, with a smile, 'This is how I like them, because it keeps them warm in winter.' And so, another nail was put into the coffin of this girl's self-esteem. A few further nails will probably be added when the girls at school start their inevitable teasing.

As adults, we are free, within the restraints of our budget and lifestyle, to please ourselves, but many of us remain 'hooked into' pleasing others. Recently, I decided to take a big step – I had my hair coloured. I had noticed a growing number of grey hairs and I didn't like the 'look'. My family thought I was being silly and said no one would notice. So I had an internal battle with myself. I knew what I wanted but there were 'old messages' in my head saying that to try to cover up grey hairs is vain, cowardly and demeaning to a liberated lady! I began to feel uncomfortable and I questioned my decision, but I'm pleased to say that the new, confident me won. I did have my hair coloured; I like it and my family think it is great. It's true that no one else has noticed, but that was hardly the point. I had it done because I had noticed. I cared and I wanted to please me.

So, find a style which you want, which helps you to feel relaxed and comfortable and which reflects the true you.

Allow yourself to be looked after from time to time

This is not last in the list because it is the 'least' – on the contrary; it is very important. It is last, because it is, perhaps, the most difficult to do without feeling guilty or inadequate! There are many reasons why this should be so. Here are a few – perhaps they will ring some bells:

- As a woman, you have grown up in a world which expects you to take the caring role (For example, it's mostly women who look after the ageing parents or in-laws; it's women who are encouraged towards the professions of nursing and social work)

- You have become used to bolstering up your fragile self-esteem by looking after others

- Taking care from others frightens you because you fear you may become totally dependent

- You have such a low opinion of yourself that you do not think anyone could freely choose to look after you

- You rate your achievements and efforts so low, that you do not think you deserve to be cared for.

Remember that old habits die hard for your friends and family as well, so they may not know that you want looking after unless you tell them! So be clear and assertive in your requests for caring; your life really is to short to waste time hanging about waiting for saints and mind-readers. Even if people genuinely care about you, they may feel slightly uncomfortable at first, but trust that, eventually, they too will get addicted to the satisfaction and pleasure which you know comes from caring for someone who needs you!

Chapter 5

Choosing the right style of behaviour

There are three broad categories of behaviour: **aggressive, passive** and **assertive.**

A confident woman can:

● Use all three behaviours

● Choose an overall style of behaviour which suits her personality and her lifestyle

● Apply the appropriate behaviour to suit each individual situation or relationship.

In my experience, people who lack confidence tend to use a limited range of behaviours and are unable to differentiate between these three styles clearly, with the consequence that their words and actions are often ineffective. You will note that the use of each behaviour has its advantages and disadvantages.

In our personal lives, each individual has to take responsibility for deciding which behaviour to use in each situation. You may, of course, choose to adapt your behaviour to suit the wishes or needs of other people, such as your family, or your boss.

In other areas of our work, the goals and values of others may also largely determine the kind of behaviour which is appropriate. For example, your organization may not expect their sales people to be passive; their secretaries to be aggressive, or, indeed, their cleaners to be assertive. Equally, as a client, you may not expect a passive barrister or an aggressive waitress, and isn't the customer always right?

Aggressive behaviour

You may not like these stereotyped roles and expectations, and you may wish to work towards effecting some changes, but in the short term you may have to work with the present day reality, if, for example, you wish to keep your job, or win your court case.

So, use the following tables as a guide to enable you to:

- Check whether you fully understand the differences between the three behaviours

- Identify the areas in your life where you may be using inappropriate behaviour

- List the changes you wish to make, putting the most difficult ones at the top of your list

- Set some realistic goals for yourself, from the bottom end of your list. One for the next month, and another for a year's time

- Share these goals with a friend, telling her – or him – how you are going to reward yourself if you achieve them.

Aggressive style of behaviour

General attitude	Domineering; forceful; attacking; insensitive; impatient; ambitious; righteous; hostile; bombastic; prejudiced; blaming; hurtful; reckless; mistrustful; status seeking; punitive
Words and phrases	'You'd better'; 'Watchout!'; 'Come on'; 'should'; 'bad'; 'stupid'; 'You!'; 'You're a typical . . .'; 'Shut-up'; 'Get out of my way'; 'Hurry up!'; 'I told you so'; 'You make me feel . . .'; 'You won't.'
Non-verbal behaviour	Clenched fists; jerky movements; finger-pointing; hands on hips; folded arms; big strides; hand thumping; back slapping; loud voice; shouting; staring; glaring; head forward; rigid; stiff
Emotions	Rage; resentment; irritation; loneliness; excitement; thrill; intoxification; passion
Sense of humour	Caustic wit; sick jokes; put-downs; teasing; bitchiness; practical jokes (but inability to laugh at self)
Lifestyle	Fast; full; competitive; many acquaintances; lack of intimacy; financially orientated; risky; short-term goals; destructive

Positive uses	Defence in the face of extreme threat; expression of justified anger; authoritative leadership in a crisis situation; good at getting noticed; able to acquire resources for a good cause
Negative consequences	The abuse of power; others are hurt; fosters aggressive and manipulative behaviour in others; encourages dependency; democracy threatened; isolation; alienation; burnout; ultimate self-destruction.

Table 5

Passive behaviour

Passive style of behaviour	
General attitude	Meek; acquiescent; compliant; submissive; long-suffering; resigned; docile; charming; helpless; self-blaming; indecisive; pessimistic

Words and phrases	'Maybe'; 'I wonder'; 'I guess'; 'Would you mind'; 'Sorry'; 'Excuse me'; 'if'; 'you know'; 'I don't know'; 'possibly'; 'I can't'; 'Later'; 'If you want'; 'If that's the way you want it'; 'It's only me'; 'Sorry to bother you'; 'I don't know what came over me'
Non-verbal behaviour	Wringing hands; fidgety movements; shuffling feet; downcast eyes; stooping; hand over mouth; whining; soft-spoken; monotonous voice; unexpressive; cute
Emotions	Fear; apprehension; anxiety; depression; guilt; hurt; bitterness; sluggishness; confusion
Sense of humour	Clowning; self-deprecating jokes; colluding with put-downs; giggliness; sarcasm; cynicism; cattiness
Lifestyle	Quiet; safe; uneventful; cautious; peaceful; nurturing; rule-bound; manipulative; hypocritical
Positive uses	Protection; discretion; avoidance of harm; reliability; low-risk; unobtrusiveness; sanctuary; modesty

Negative consequences	Victimization; powerlessness; martyrdom; being an object of persecution; becoming a gossip; developing phobias and obsessions, depression, boredom, apathy; being overworked; becoming ill; losing self-respect; seeking attention covertly; courting humiliation and neglect

Table 6

Assertive behaviour

Assertive style of behaviour	
General attitudes	Optimistic; positive; thoughtful; rational; evaluative; respectful; encouraging; sensible; fair-minded; sensitive; compromising; self-protective; insistent; decisive; sincere

Words and phrases	'I want'; 'I feel'; 'I don't like'; 'Let's'; 'What do you think?'; 'How can we resolve this?'; 'Let's discuss'; 'The alternatives/options are . . .'; 'I won't'; 'No'; 'Yes'; 'I love you'; 'I know that'; 'I appreciate that you . . .'
Non-verbal behaviour	Expressive; relaxed, steady posture; upright; direct eye contact; strong, clear voice; energetic
Emotions	Happy; sad; angry; compassionate; calm; serene; poised
Sense of humour	Playful; fun-loving; willing to laugh at own behaviour; witty, but not at the expense of others
Lifestyle	Active; varied; dynamic; innovative; organized; purposeful; ethical; humanitarian; conscientious
Positive uses	Decisive; active; organized; efficient; team spirited; democratic; independent; creative; able to manage successfully; effective at communicating; able to cope with criticism; intimate; able to take calculated risks
Negative consequences	Dislike from some people; limited power; restricted wealth; repercussions from mistakes; burdened with other peoples' high expectations and demands.

Table 7

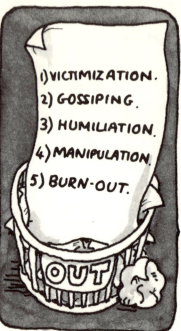

Chapter 6

Becoming more assertive

Your right to be assertive

Based on the evidence of both my personal and professional experiences, my guess is that your goals include behaving more assertively. Most people who lack confidence rely too heavily on the passive and aggressive behaviours. Somewhere in your life, past or present, you are responding to the injunction: 'You have no right to be assertive'.

The first step is to replace this with your own set of rights. Table 8 on page 78 lists the 12 basic human rights which I use in my assertiveness training courses. Many people say this list alone has changed their lives. If you know it by heart when you are in a situation which requires assertive behaviour, you will be reminded and reassured by recalling the appropriate right.

Remember, though, that these are human rights for everyone, so as an assertive woman, you encourage others to live by these rights and you respect their privilege to do so.

Also, as a self-confident woman, you should be able to look critically at this list and, if it does not suit your values, adapt it, or compile your own. You should feel secure enough in yourself to tolerate differences in people, as long as they are not hurting or abusing others. Not everyone may wish to be as assertive as you are!

If you are sure of your rights you will be better able to tolerate the inevitable put-downs from those around you who may be feeling the consequences of your changed behaviour. Adrian

Mole's reaction in Sue Townsend's book, *The Secret Diary of Adrian Mole Aged Thirteen and Three Quarters* (Methuen, 1982) is fairly typical:

My mother has gone to a woman's workshop on assertiveness training. Men aren't allowed. I asked my father what 'assertiveness training' is. He said 'God knows, but whatever it is, it's bad news for me . . .' Then my mother came home and started bossing us around. She said, 'The worm has turned,' and 'Things are going to be different around here,' and things like that. Then she went into the kitchen and started making a chart dividing all the housework into three . . .

Assertive rights

1 The right to ask for what we want (realizing that the other person has a right to say 'No').

2 The right to have an opinion, feelings and emotions and to express them appropriately.

3 The right to make statements which have no logical basis, and which we do not have to justify.

4 The right to make our own decisions and cope with the consequences.

5 The right to choose whether or not to get involved with the problems of someone else.

6 The right not to know about something, or to understand.

7 The right to make mistakes.

8 The right to be successful.

9 The right to change our mind.

10 The right to privacy.

11 The right to be alone and independent.

12 The right to change ourselves and be assertive people.

NB The assertive person is not just concerned about his or her own rights but always encourages and promotes assertiveness in others.

Table 8

Being persistent

Perhaps, one of the most common problems people in my groups experience is an inability to be persistent in asserting their needs and wants, even in the face of extreme injustice.

Do you:

- give in too easily when someone disagrees with you?
- 'Blow your top' too readily?
- Secretly resort to 'behind-the-back' techniques?

If so, you will probably find it useful to use one of the techniques we use in assertiveness training. It is called **Broken Record**. This means repeating over and over again, in an assertive and relaxed manner, what it is you want or need, until the other person gives in, or agrees to negotiate with you. It is particularly effective if you use it in conjunction with an **empathic statement** – in other words, one which indicates to the other person that you have considered their position, point of view or feelings. For example, you bought a pair of shoes at a shop last Saturday. On the second occasion you wore them, the heel came loose as you were walking home. You wish to return them to the shop and obtain a refund. You want the cash, as you know there are no other shoes of your size in that shop and you wish to spend the money elsewhere. You do not want to waste your precious lunch hour arguing with sales assistants, especially when you are so sure of your rights. Neither do you want to end up 'rescuing' them because you feel sorry for them. In similar circumstances, in the past, you have always been seduced into taking a credit note, or buying some alternative goods in the shop, so you decide to use assertive techniques.

You think of a concise, clear sentence which outlines your needs and you rehearse saying it before venturing forth. ('I would like my money back today please'.) Prior to entering the shop, you take some nice deep breaths and relax your muscles, thinking of the reward you have promised yourself if you succeed.

Your exchange with the shop manager may sound like this:

You   'I bought these shoes here last Saturday, and I have worn them twice. The heel is coming off and I would like my money back today, please.'

Manager	'You must have given them a hard time. This has never happened to these shoes before.'
You	'I appreciate that you are surprised at this happening, but I have only worn these shoes twice and the heel is coming off, I would like my money back today, please.'
Manager	'Well, they're probably not the right size for you. Did you buy them in a hurry?'
You	'I have only worn them twice, and you can see that the heel is coming off. I would like my money back today, please.'
Manager	'We have the new autumn stock arriving in the next few days. I'll give you a credit note and personally help you choose a pair that fit.
You	'I understand that you are concerned to avoid losing a sale, but I would like my money back today, please.'
Manager	'You'll find that stocks are low in all the shops at the moment. It's not our fault; there's been a transport drivers' strike. You'd be well advised to wait until next week. We hold the biggest range of this kind of shoe in town.'
You	'I can see that things have been difficult for you, but I would like my money back today, please.'
Manager	'Well, if you insist. How much were they?'

At the end of this transaction, you have achieved what you wanted and had a right to have, but the manager isn't very pleased; you might not even get a smile from him. Only you can decide whether or not you paid too high a price for being assertive!

There are many other situations where the broken record method can be used effectively, including at home and at work, but it is not infallible, because one of the factors we cannot control is the other person's value system. This may mean that you are dealing with someone who also believes that they are in the right and will not back down or someone who doesn't care whether you are right.

In the latter case, you have the choice of trying the same, or other assertive techniques, with someone in a more senior position than the manager, or resorting to passive or aggressive behaviour if you feel you are justified to do so.

In the former case, you may wish to work towards a fair compromise, so here are some useful tips to help you negotiate with confidence.

Successful negotiation

- **Relax** – Use relaxation techniques to help you keep calm

- **Empathize** – Make a statement which indicates that you understand and have considered their point of view and their feelings

- **Clarify** – Ask for any information you may require about their argument

- **Prepare** – Do your homework thoroughly; gather together any facts and figures which may support your case

- **Be concise** – Keep to the point; use the Broken Record method to bring the argument back on track, if necessary

- **Compromise** – Don't be stubborn and wait for the other person to give in first; offer a reasonable compromise.

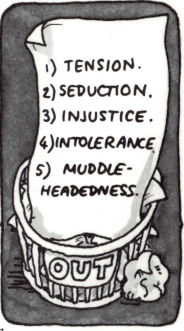

Chapter 7

Good communication

Confident people are not necessarily all brilliant, charismatic orators, but they do understand the importance of good communication and are prepared to work on their weaknesses to ensure that they have effective skills.

Let's summarize the main points which have been made in previous chapters about communication.

- Self-knowledge and self-awareness enable us to have more control over our behaviour, including our communication patterns

- We need to ensure that the part of our personality (that is, the Parent, Adult or Child) we are using complements that of the person to whom we are conveying our message

- The styles of behaviour we choose [i.e. passive, aggressive or assertive] must be appropriate to the situation and the relationship.

Here are some additional areas which I have found helpful to cover in confidence-building programmes.

The art of conversation

Having to start and maintain a conversation is the nightmare of many people who lack confidence. Perhaps some of these common 'avoidance' tricks which people have shared with me are familiar to you, such as crossing the road to avoid someone, choosing an empty train compartment, choosing to shop during quiet periods, not going to parties, saying 'no' to a new date, not joining clubs, choosing a hobby which requires solitude or staying in a boring job to avoid working in an environment which involves socializing.

The following suggestions may be useful:

Never underestimate 'small talk'

Small talk is an invaluable 'warm-up' for the more serious and satisfying conversations. It gives us some breathing space in which to relax and enables us to gain a useful impression of the other person's basic attitudes and values. So, start collecting your stories about the weather! People lacking in confidence often make the mistake of being too earnest and asking personal questions too soon. Both are habits born out of compulsive desires to please and to divert the attention away from themselves.

Choose a conversation opener which is safe and doesn't run much risk of you getting rebuffed. A question or statement which is personal can be perceived as threatening.

- **Low risk openers** – 'It's very warm today,' 'There are lots of people here, aren't there?' and 'The train is now half an hour late.'

- **Higher risk openers** – 'What brings you here today?' 'You don't seem to be the kind of person I would expect to find here,' and 'You caught my eye as soon as you walked in. Are you on your own?'

Develop your listening skills

Over-anxiety tends to make us interrupt too early and too often. For example:

Joan 'Last week . . . when I was in Bristol . . .'

Mary 'Oh, Bristol. That's a place I've never been to. Is it nice?'

Mary is attempting to be warm and friendly but, in her anxiety to demonstrate this, she has cut off Joan's attempt to tell her story. She may have been responding to a slight pause on Joan's part, which could also have been attributed to anxiety.

A more skilled way of 'filling the gap', would have been to say, 'Oh, you were in Bristol, were you?' This is **reflective listening** and indicates that you are attending. You simply repeat back to the talker, maybe in slightly different words, a summary of what she, or he, has just said. You can also use it to check out that you have correctly heard and understood what the other person has said. This is encouraging for the talker because it demonstrates your interest in what she or he is saying. It is a skill used by counsellors and good chat show hosts – watch out for it! But don't use it if you are having difficulty in getting a word in edgeways!

Remember, confident people do not hog a conversation and can rest comfortably with silence.

> *The trouble with telling a good story is that it inevitably reminds the other fellow of a bad one.*
>
> Sid Caesar

Be positive

'Ain't it awful' conversations become very tedious and boring after a while, but don't go to the other extreme and play 'jolly hockey sticks'!

Use humour

But stick to the assertive style. Develop this lighter side of your personality, and build up a repertoire of funny stories. Make a conscious choice to watch more comedy on TV or at the theatre.

Watch out for non-verbal signals

Approximately 75 per cent of communication is transmitted through body language. In any crowd, you can spot a shy person by looking for the expressionless faces and rigid postures. Start with becoming more expressive yourself. Allow your body the freedom to communicate what you are feeling – within reason, of course! Join a dance or mime class if you need extra help.

Select the appropriate tone of voice to suit your message,

because this will have more impact than the actual words which you use. Think of the many different tones you can use to say 'It's good to see you here, today,' when you meet someone unexpectedly at a conference or school function. People lacking in confidence might say this with a meek, hesitant voice, or, alternatively, with an overpowering, cheery tone. A confident person will tend to use the middle range of their voice. If the statement is being made at an informal party a different tone would be more appropriate.

Be aware of your smiles. Women often smile too much when they are nervous, especially in the company of men. Most of us have received 'put-down' comments such as 'Give us a smile, love'; and 'Don't look so glum, it may never happen,' when we were trying to have a serious conversation. The result is that when we are making an effort to have a friendly conversation we may tend to over-smile in an effort to please. Of course we shouldn't go to the other extreme and take on a stony face, but if we want to be taken more seriously, we must change our smiling habits.

Use eye contact well. If you want to hold someone's attention, look them directly in the eye but don't stare or hold their gaze for too long. For most conversations people tend to feel comfortable with eye contact for about 50 per cent of the time.

Select your questions

Remember that the way you phrase a question will often determine the response it receives. Use tables 3 and 4 on pages 52-4 to help you become more aware of the different kinds of questions you could use and to check whether you are using them to your best advantage.

Use self-disclosure appropriately

Research has shown that sharing information about yourself and your feelings is a way of moving a relationship forward towards intimacy. Decide whether or not this is what you want from the relationship, or what the 'contract' between you ought to be. Do you want a close friendship with your colleagues, your neighbours or your hairdresser, or do you want to set some boundaries? Remember that if someone else decides to share their love-life with you, you are not duty-bound to do the same in return. You have a right to defend your personal space.

You must also take into account the cultural background of the person talking to you and show some respect and understanding of their pattern with regard to self-disclosure. For example, men who are used to operating in a very 'macho' world will not be comfortable with personal revelations. Their only experience of any kind of intimacy may be within close sexual encounters, so self-disclosure may well have associations with these kinds of relationships. If you know that this is not the kind of relationship you want with a particular man, do not self-disclose or respond to any probing he may do with his questions.

Giving and receiving compliments

Fan You were superb in Romeo and Juliet.
Actor I'll bet you say that to everyone who is superb.

To watch two shy people trying to give each other compliments can be an excruciatingly painful experience. Perhaps you have had first-hand experience of it. Watching two assertive people do the same thing can, by contrast, be moving and uplifting.

So what is the difference? Apart from the obvious self-esteem problems, which we have discussed earlier, the difference is that one pair has learned the art, and the other has not. Once you have learned the basics you tend to get a good deal of practice. *Genuine* compliment sharing is contagious and addictive. The more you give the more you are likely to get back; the more you receive them assertively, the more you will receive; the more you feel their benefit, the more likely you are to want your 'daily dose', so the more compliments you give – and so it goes on!

If all this sounds sickening and self-indulgent, then perhaps you have been starved, or fed on the wrong mixture! Before collapsing in a heap of nausea and embarrassment, try using the following guidelines.

Giving compliments

● **Relax** – If you know that you are going to approach someone to give them a compliment, and are feeling nervous, take some slow, deep breaths and give your body a bit of a shake. The compliment is much more likely to be received without embarrassment if you are not looking, and feeling, terrified!

- **Choose the right time and place** – Many people are so embarrassed about giving compliments that they tend to slip them in when they are situated in a place where it's difficult for people to react well, or when they are just rushing off somewhere. Don't give compliments when it's obvious, from the mood of the other person, that they are not going to be well received. For example, if someone has just received some unexpected bad news, they would prefer your sympathy, or empathy; they don't need to be told that their hair is looking nice today, or that they did really well in last year's exams.

- **Keep good eye-contact** – I know I don't hear too well the compliments which are addressed to my shoes!

- **Be specific** – General compliments are often not very useful and less credible. It means much more to say: 'I really like the way that you handled that meeting yesterday,' than 'I think you are really good at your job,' or 'You always manage to select colours which complement your hair and eyes,' than 'You've got good dress sense.'

- **Don't idolize** – It's not comfortable standing on a pedestal, and people will eventually get irritated with you if you try to keep them up there. So cut down on the frequency of 'over-the-top' adulations such as 'Oh, you're absolutely wonderful and amazing and fabulous and magnificent and sensational and brilliant and miraculous and . . .'

- **Don't include a put-down of you** – This is a common fault of people lacking in confidence. For example, they may say: 'You're such a nice person. I wish I were like you,' or 'This is a wonderful meal, I'm a terrible cook.' How can anyone enjoy your compliment when they are being manipulatively hooked into rescuing you!

- **Don't include a put-down of the other person** – Many compliments have a sting in the tail. (Usually caused by a build-up of unexpressed resentment.) For example, 'Well done for clearing the table, I didn't think I'd ever see the day!' or 'You look really nice today. It's good to see you in something new.'

Receiving compliments

- **Smile but don't giggle** – Allow yourself the pleasure of having your self-esteem boosted

- **Maintain eye contact** – Resist the temptation to avert your eyes as soon as you hear a compliment approaching

- **Listen without interrupting** – Many people cut off a compliment in its prime

- **Don't respond with a put-down of you** – For example, 'You wouldn't say that if you could see me at home,' or 'Well, it's about time I got something right, isn't it?'

- **Don't dismiss the compliment** – For example, 'Well, actually I've had it years,' or 'It wasn't very difficult anyway.'

- **Don't smother the compliment immediately with a 'retaliation'** – 'Well, I think you're marvellous as well,' or 'You do just as good a job as I do.' Your compliment may be interpreted for what it probably is, that is, an attempt to cope with your embarrassment. Allow the dust to settle and then you can give your compliment

- **Ask for clarification** – If you do not undertand the compliment, or it's too general, ask the giver to be more specific. For example, 'What was it about the way I gave that speech that you thought was good?' or 'Is it the way the room is decorated, or is it the furniture, or anything else you particularly like about it?'

- **Say 'thank-you' assertively** – Don't be over-effusive with the thanks. For example, 'Oh, that was really kind of you to say that. You do say some lovely things. You're wonderful!' A simple 'thank you' and a smile is usually all that is required.

Making requests

Bear the following points in mind when you are thinking about making requests:

- **Be sure of your rights and values** – Doing your homework before you make your request will help you to assume an overall confident manner. Have evidence of your rights at hand if necessary. Be sure you really do want what you are asking for

- **Be positive** – Don't go into the situation expecting that your request will be refused. I have learned so much from my husband about taking a positive, optimistic attitude. His training as a salesperson has taught him that a negative attitude is disastrous. Time and time again when I find myself in a mood where I feel there's no point, he has made me realize that I am predetermining the outcome. So if you have little to lose from asking, ask positively

- **Be concise** – We are all less receptive to requests which come wrapped in reams of unnecessary packaging. So get to the point as soon as possible and don't waste time with endless justifications and apologies

- **Be persistent** – Use the Broken Record method to keep you on track, and be ready to resist side arguments. Don't get emotional. You have already checked out your rights and values

- **Be polite** – Be sure that you know the appropriate protocol. You don't necessarily have to overdose on 'humble pie' but people lacking in confidence sometimes have led such a sheltered existence that they have not had the advantage of 'learning the rules'. Each society, culture, sub-culture and generation has its accepted method of making requests. You don't necessarily have to play their game 'by the book' but it does make sense to make allowances for it. Repeated social gaffes will not help your cause

- **Rehearse** – I find the assertiveness training technique of **Scripting** an invaluable tool for making both written and

Scripting

A useful way of preparing your 'opening speech', so that you can make an impact and start assertively. Use it on any occasion when you know you are likely to feel intimidated or will be in danger of getting side-tracked. It can also be a very useful model for composing short concise, 'punchy' letters.

Use the following sentence to remind you of the various stages.

EVEN FISH NEED CONFIDENCE

Explanation
- Explain the situation as you see it
- Be as objective as possible
- Keep to the point
- Be brief
- Don't theorize or play 'amateur psychologist'

(One sentence should generally be sufficient.)

Feelings
- Acknowledge your own (— but don't accuse the other person of making you feel anything!)
- Empathize with the other person, or persons

Needs
- Say what you want
- Be selective — one need at a time, if possible
- Offer a compromise, if appropriate

Consequences
- Outline the 'pay off' for the other person i.e. the 'reward', if they should comply with your wishes.
- Note, in brackets, what would happen if they do not do what you ask i.e. the 'punishment'. (It helps you to be more assertive if you know what power you have in the situation.)

Table 9

Examples of Scripts

N.B. Always use the 'reward', if possible, first. Only use the threat of 'punishment', if all else fails.

1 For the last few months your expense claims have been late. (**explanation**) I am getting very irritated about this although I appreciate that you do not like doing paperwork. (**feelings**) In future would you please make sure they reach my desk by the last day of each month (**needs**) and then I won't be continually nagging you and we'll get on much better. (**consequences** — *Reward*) [If you do not, I will have to discuss the matter with the manager. (**consequences** — *Punishment*)]

2 I have cooked the evening meal every night for the past month (**explanation**) and I am getting very fed up as a result. I know that you are very busy at work at the moment (**feelings**) but I would like you to do your fair share of the cooking (**needs**) and then perhaps I'll feel less tired and more interested in going out with you. (**consequences** — *Reward*) [If you don't I shall merely cook for myself. (**consequences** — *Punishment*)]

Table 10

verbal requests. The technique is outlined in Table 9 on page 90 and a sample script can be found in Table 10 above. A fuller explanation of this technique can be found in my book *Assert yourself* (Thorsons, 1986).

If it is a verbal request, script what you are going to say and then practise saying it out loud so that you can hear what it sounds like and can add colour to it by varying your tone of voice.

If you anticipate a good deal of opposition to your request, ask a friend to do a role play with you. You can tell them to come up with all the arguments you are likely to meet and then you can practise, using both your scripting and broken record techniques.

The art of public speaking

This is an art which now, with the upsurge in self-advocacy, is no longer practised by a privileged few. In an article in the *Guardian* (31 August, 1988), I was very impressed to read that the mentally handicapped self-advocacy movement is gaining in strength. It described how one woman called Christine is now feeling confident enough to go out and talk to conferences and lead workshops.

There are now many excellent books and courses on this subject, so I will only list a few important points:

- **Be prepared** – Make notes, preferably on a series of cards, but do not learn your speech by heart, or read it. Remember to include an introduction, which outlines the gist of what you will say and finish with a summary of your main points. Rehearse in front of a mirror, or with a friend

- **Relax** – Wear comfortable clothing (not a brand new outfit which you may feel very self-conscious in). Do some slow, deep breathing just before entering the room, and think of an image which you find relaxing. Stand tall with the full support of *two* feet, positioned slightly apart. Use your face and your eyes to communicate non-verbally, rather than gesticulating too freely with your hands

- **Introduce yourself positively** – 'Unaccustomed as I am to public speaking' jokes are a put-down of you and are very boring. It's fine to acknowledge your nervousness but don't give the impression that you really would prefer to be under the table. Indicate to your audience that you are pleased to be speaking to them, in spite of your terror

- **Watch the tone of your voice** – Pitch your voice low. Women tend to have high voices which can become difficult to listen to after a while. Vary your tone as much as possible because nervousness can make our voices sound very monotonous. If you find your voice becoming 'squeaky', pause for a moment, take a slow, deep breath, swallow gently and take a sip of water, if you find that helps. If you have never heard your voice, record it on a good quality tape recorder and listen to it. Remember that even if you are like me and don't wish to believe this truth, the sound you will hear *is* the sound others hear!

- **Smile** – Research has shown that it can help both you to relax and your audience to warm to you. Use *assertive* humour to help you. But be aware of over-smiling, or using coy or seductive smiles

- **Make eye contact** – Make eye contact with as many people in the audience as you can without distracting yourself too much

- **Acknowledge and respond to audience reaction** – But use your notes to help you to get back on track. Trust that the audience would rather hear your important points than improvized waffle. Use the broken record technique to deal,

in an assertive manner, with unwanted interruptions. If you are having difficulty gauging the audience's reaction, ask for feedback but, do so assertively. There is a big difference between saying 'Am I boring you?' and 'I'd like to check out whether I am covering the points that are of interest to you.'

- **Use visual and other aids** – If you are very nervous or unused to public speaking, it may help to have the focus taken off you for a moment and give you the breathing space in which to regain your confident composure

- **Finish positively** – Again beware of being a 'creep' by using statements which are a put-down of you. For example, 'I hope I haven't bored you,' or 'Thank you for listening so patiently to me. I think you all deserve a break now.' But it is OK to compliment them assertively and share the pleasure you experienced in talking to them, for example, 'You have been a very attentive audience and I have enjoyed talking to you,' or, 'You have been a very challenging audience and I have found talking to you very stimulating.'

Chapter 8
Anger and criticism

Handling criticism

People who lack confidence rarely give direct criticism to others. They sit and sulk, bitch behind backs or resort to violence. Equally they rarely hear direct criticism of themselves. They either deafen themselves and others with self-criticism, so no one else gets a word in edgeways, or they play 'goody-gumdrops' so skilfully that people think they are much too nice to hurt. The end result is that they are often shocked and surprised when they are rejected. They cannot understand why they didn't get the promotion, why their partner wants to leave them, why their children have stopped coming at Christmas or, why there are so few people at their death-bed!

Golden rules for receiving criticism

> *No one can make you feel inferior without your consent.*
> *Eleanor Roosevelt*

- **Anticipate** – Your self-development work should have made you more aware of the kind of things you are likely to be criticized about. Continue to ask for feedback on your work and general behaviour but do so assertively. Don't invite a put-down or false reassurance, such as 'Am I doing this badly?'

- **Keep calm** – Check your body for tension; take some slow controlled breaths

- **Think positively** – What the other person is saying *may* be useful feedback for you. Assertive people are not afraid of making mistakes and view them as a useful learning experience

- **Stay in your Adult** – The Adult is the part of your personality which can be rational and objective. Judge whether this criticism is a) being given by someone whose opinion you value and b) whether it is fair and constructive. Use your Adult to remind you that it is aspects of your behaviour which are being criticized and it need not be a total rejection of you

- **Listen carefully** – Calmly reflect back to your critic what he or she has just said to a) demonstrate that you are listening and b) to check that you have heard correctly. (Anxiety can certainly impair our perceptive abilities temporarily, if not our actual hearing.)

- **Empathize with your critic** – But don't sympathize with a put-down of you! (For example, 'It must be awful, having to live with someone like me.') Say something like, 'I can see that what I am doing is upsetting/frustrating you,' or 'I understand that you have not been happy for some time with . . .'

- **Play for time** – Play for time if necessary, especially if you feel yourself slipping out of your Adult, perhaps getting too scared or angry. Ask to meet later, suggest that you will then be able to listen more attentively to what they are saying. You will then have a chance to calm down, review the facts and, if necessary, prepare your counter attack

- **Protect yourself** – Use the self-protective assertiveness skills outlined in Table 11 on page 98 to block criticism. You may wish to do this because a) you have judged the critic is being unfair and abusive to you, or b) the time or place may not be appropriate or convenient for you to be having this 'conversation'. For example, you may be trying to reserve your strength for an important meeting, you may be in a public place or you may be tired

- **Ask for clarification** – Use the technique of negative enquiry, described in Table 11 to get more information. Using this technique has the added advantage of uncovering destructive, put-down behaviour which comes disguised as a caring enquiry or an inocuous question, for example, 'Have you bought a new lipstick?' (meaning 'That lipstick looks awful on you.') or 'Was there a lot of traffic on the road?' (meaning 'You're late again. You're always late.')

- **Share your reaction** – React to constructive criticism honestly, unless you have a special reason for not wishing to do so. Acknowledge the positive aspects. Say, for example, 'I feel a bit knocked out by what you have just said, but it has given me something to think about,' or 'I feel very hurt at the moment, but I'm glad you actually said what you said,' or 'It's been very useful for me to hear what you think, even though I cannot agree with it.'

- **Give your inner confidence a boost** – Remind yourself of your own worth, your own values, the progress you are making and ask for support from the people in your life who love you, warts and all

- **Work out an action plan if necessary** – If the criticism has been valid and you want to change your behaviour, work out how you are going to do it. If the criticism was destructive and you don't agree with it but are still hurt and immobilized by it, plan to rehearse your self-protective techniques, or plan to explore the root cause of your reaction. For example, the critic may have reminded you of your Mum, your Dad or your boss at work. This insight may be enough to 'free' you or you may need to do some other self-development work on these other relationships so that they do not continue to depower you. Seek help from a professional counsellor or therapist if you remain mystified by your own behaviour.

Self-protective techniques for coping with criticism

Fogging
Calmly acknowledge that there *may* be some truth in what the critic has just said.

(N.B. You do not let them know whether you really agree with them. In this way your critic doesn't quite know what to make of the situation and has nothing to 'feed' off. Use this technique whenever you want to play very safe, especially with people who do not share your values. It can also be used within close relationships when you are being unfairly criticized and you do not wish to defend yourself at that particular point in time — maybe you are too tired or too busy.)

Examples:
1   Critic: 'You're looking peaky today.'
     Reply: 'Perhaps I'm not looking at my best today.'
2   Critic: 'Your children really are spoilt.'
     Reply: 'Maybe I am a bit too liberal with them sometimes.'

Negative assertion
Calmly agree with the truth in the criticism.

(N.B. Use only with people with whom you feel it is appropriate to share your faults and mistakes.)

Examples:
1   Critic: 'Your room is a disgrace!'
     Reply: 'Yes, I'm not a very tidy person.'
2   Critic: 'You are the world's worst cook!'
     Reply: 'You are right, I am not very good at cooking.'

Negative enquiry
Ask for clarification, or for further criticism.

(N.B. Use only when you are feeling very confident. If your critic launches into further abuse, use Fogging to stop him/her.)

Examples:
1   Critic: 'I don't think you'll ever make a manager, the way you behave.'
     Reply: 'What exactly is it about my behaviour which makes you say that?'
2   Critic: 'That colour looks awful on you.'
     Reply: 'Do you think that I usually wear clothes which do not suit me?'

Table 11

Golden rules for giving criticism

- **Choose an appropriate time and place** – Your criticism is less likely to be heard if it was given when the other person is feeling vulnerable or powerless. If possible give the other person a warning, such as, 'There are a few things about your work which I would like to discuss with you. Could we meet at lunchtime?'

- **Keep calm** – Relax before starting to speak

- **Keep in your Adult** – This is the part of your personality in which you can be rational and objective

- **Be optimistic** – Tell yourself that the other person may be pleased to have had feedback from you. If you go into the situation expecting a fight, you are more likely to get it. Your body signals (for example, rigid posture and staring eyes) may give away that you are braced for a fight, even though you have chosen your words with care

- **Acknowledge the positive** – If you can include some genuine positive statement, do so. For example, 'Before I begin I would like to say how much I like working with you,' or 'I know that you are trying really hard . . .' or 'I know that you do love me, and that's wonderful . . .'

- **Empathize** – Indicate that you have considered their position and/or feelings. For example, 'This must be a very difficult job for you' or 'I appreciate that you are working within a limited budget,' or 'I know that what I am saying must be hurtful.'

- **Be specific** – Don't generalize. For example, say, 'You haven't done the washing up for three days,' rather than, 'You never help me.' Say, 'You ring me too often,' rather than, 'You're too demanding.'

- **Keep to the point** – Don't use this as an opportunity to dump a backlog of garbage. Use the Broken Record technique to bring the other person back on track, if necessary

- **Focus on behaviour** – Don't attack the whole person. For example, say, 'I think your manner on the phone yesterday was rude,' rather than, 'You're such a rude person.' Say, 'I don't like the way you fondle me while we are trying to have a serious conversation,' rather than, 'You're a sex maniac.'

- **Don't label or stereotype** – Labelling someone is a put-down. For example, don't say 'You're a typical man,' 'All you Tories . . .' 'Kids are all the same these days.'

- **Be realistic in your requests** – Don't expect someone to change the habits of a lifetime overnight. Don't ask for a complete personality transformation or for resources which they don't have access to

- **Outline the consequences** – As in Scripting (see page 90), let the other person know, without using a threatening or aggressive tone, what he or she stands to gain if they change their behaviour or, alternatively, what they are likely to lose if they do not.

Managing anger assertively

Anger is the natural reaction we experience when we feel threatened or frustrated. Psychologist Colleen Kelley writes:

Anger is the first emotion human beings experience and the last one we learn to manage effectively. As early as four months of age, the human infant's vague feelings of distress differentiate into recognizable anger; for many of us, a lifetime is spent denying, suppressing, displacing, or avoiding this troublesome emotional experience.

I would add that this is an area which women have, traditionally, found more difficult than men. We have been brought up often to believe that it is better to 'do anything to keep the peace'. These are the kinds of messages women I know recall having been given, either directly or indirectly, in their childhood:

- Nice girls don't respond with aggression
- An angry face is an ugly face
- Being the weaker sex, girls get hurt if they fuel the fire

- Girls should try to understand and help the angry person

- Girls can be more effective using behind-the-scene tactics.

Boys, on the other hand, have been encouraged to develop and test their manhood in the field of conflict from a very early age. As a result, they are usually well acquainted with both their own and other people's anger by the time they reach manhood. Some of them are obviously better than others at managing this emotion, but at least it is generally recognized that they have some anger to manage!

The problem for some women may be even more difficult if they were brought up in a family or culture where anger was generally frowned upon. They might have received an overdose of messages such as these:

- Love thine enemy

- Anger restrained is wisdom gained

- Anger is a brief madness

- Anger makes dull men witty but makes them poor.

They may have had some traumatic experiences of being hurt by mismanaged anger. Perhaps they were at the receiving end of an adult losing control and have therefore grown up with an understandable terror of anger.

Alternatively, they may have had their own justifiable anger repressed when they were powerless to fight back. Perhaps their natural temper tantrums at three years old were mismanaged. Many parents feel very threatened by their children's behaviour at this age and may, as a consequence, overreact. Or maybe their natural rebelliousness during teenage years was stifled or met with overpowering violence.

So the reasons why we may have a problem in this area are probably complex and manifold and we may have to work quite hard over a long period of time to counteract the unhealthy messages. But it is worth doing. An assertive confident woman must be able to cope with anger because:

- She does not 'play safe' and therefore she will inevitably meet strong feelings from opposition sooner or later

- She has a well-developed sense of her own values and knows what she wants, so she is likely to respond to injustices and frustration with strong feelings.

Angela Molnos, a psychotherapist, suggests in her book *Anger that Destroys and the Anger that Heals* (Sage, 1986), that there are two kinds of anger which we have to recognize.

- **Healing anger** – This is expressed at the time it arises, towards the person who triggered it off, and in connection with the issue which triggered it off.

- **Destructive anger** – This is expressed too late, is displaced, and gets connected with a cover-up issue.

During the last few years, I have run many workshops and courses on this subject and I have seen very many people take gargantuan steps forward in terms of confidence, as a result of learning to manage anger more effectively. Using the exercises in Section two to help you, work patiently through some of these tried and tested stages:

Become aware of your own anger

Interestingly, many people first show an interest in courses because people around them are getting angry and they are aware of their inability to cope effectively. The feelings which they are aware of in themselves are depression, anxiety and fear. They are rarely aware of, or in contact with, their own anger.

Manage anger assertively

If they do get angry then it often happens when they are least expecting it and they cannot make sense of it. Remember that depression is merely anger turned in against yourself, instead of being directed outwards.

It's often easier to identify your minor frustrations first. Try listing things which irritate you for a week and then try making a note of the things which annoy you. You may find some common themes running through them, such as injustice, which may give you a clue as to what you yourself are angry about. Perhaps you are suppressing your feelings concerning a major injustice you and others are experiencing.

Discover your personal reasons for not expressing anger

This may mean reflecting on your childhood and/or your current relationships and lifestyle. Start by asking yourself how your parents handled their anger. Are you still carrying their flag?

Assess the price you are paying for being too 'nice'

This may include not getting genuine feedback which could be useful for your personal growth; you could be stifling the growth of others around you, such as your children or the people who work for you; you may be limiting the potential for intimacy in certain relationships. These kinds of relationships need a fuse which can be blown at regular intervals, otherwise they stagnate or 'blow-up'. A good row often brings people closer and that's why 'making up' has earned its reputation of being good fun!

Finally, we now know that repressing anger is a contributory factor in many physical illnesses. These range from headaches to heart disease and cancer.

Learn to express your anger assertively

Starting always with the minor frustrations. (Follow the guidelines in Table 12 on page 104.)

Learn to respond assertively to anger in others

Starting with low-risk situations first. (See Table 13, page 105.)

Release residual physical tension

When we get angry our body springs into action to prepare us for the fight. If this 'fight' doesn't take place (and, luckily, they rarely do in a civilized society), we are often left with a build up of tension. It is very important to have an outlet. Men have traditionally used sport and 'horse-play' for this purpose. As women who are learning to get angry, we too must have our outlets. Thumping a cushion, though helpful, is sometimes not sufficient.

Dealing with your own anger

- **Own your feeling** – Acknowledge and claim by using 'I' statements. For example, say, 'I am angry/frustrated/irritated,' and not 'It makes me mad,' or 'You've made me furious.' Remember that no one, and no situation, has the power to make you feel anything. One person may be incensed by certain behaviour, another person may be able to take or leave it. Owning your anger helps you to feel more in control of it

- **Judge the level of anger** – Be aware of your differing degrees of anger; listen to the 'symptoms' in your body which may give you a clue as to whether you are furious or mildly irritated. Knowing the level of anger helps us to assess our capacity to deal with it

- **Diagnose the threat** – What do I stand to lose?; why am I feeling frustrated? This diagnosis often simply reveals a difference in values, upbringing, or opinion. The real threat may be minimal; the 'fantasy' may be to do with a past hurt

- **Share the threat** – Share it as it is experienced by you. For example, 'I feel as though you are trying to control me'; 'I feel as though I will be left to cope with every-

---

thing on my own in the end.' Sharing helps diffuse the feeling and gives you an opportunity to get some feedback

- **Physically express the feeling** – Try to do this if it is appropriate to do so, and if you can without, of course, hurting anyone. Relearn how to stamp your feet, slam a door, bang a table, throw a cushion and shout. If you cannot release this tension at the time of getting angry, find an outlet later, or you may end up attacking the innocent, for example, kicking the cat; screaming at the kids or picking a fight with someone you love

- **Forgive** – You cannot truly reach this stage until you have expressed your anger and understood it. It's tempting to think we can skip the uncomfortable stages, but if we do, the feelings have a nasty habit of backfiring on us. They are stored in our unconscious as resentment, or guilt, and they can play havoc with our health and our relationships. If you can *truly* 'wipe the slate clean', this magnanimous gesture can do wonders for your self-esteem. You will earn respect from yourself as well as others.

Table 12

Dealing with another's anger

- **Acknowledge the other person's feeling** – Say 'I can see that you are angry.' This will help diffuse the feeling; they no longer have to shout and scream abuse at you; they know their message has been received and understood! If you ignore the feeling, it is likely to become intensified

- **Acknowledge your own feeling** – Let the other person know how your defensiveness may affect your judgement and behaviour. For example, say, 'I'm feeling very frightened and I don't think I can talk to you in this state,' or 'I'm also getting angry and I don't think I can think clearly about what you are saying, while I am feeling like this.'

- **Broken record** – Use a statement such as, 'If you calm down I will listen to you,' or repeat their name. This will help you to keep control of your feelings as well as to get the attention of the other person

- **Clarify and diagnose** – Give and request feedback. Use negative enquiry (see page 98) to get more information. You may want them to be more specific or to tell you if there is anything else about your behaviour which they are upset about. Ask what the other person, needs, wants and expects

- **Re-negotiate the relationship** – So many people make the mistake of trying to get things back to how they were before. 'Before' was probably not very satisfactory and that may have been why the other person was angry. Unless you wish to have the same old argument time and time again (as happens in many marriages) the relationship must be re-negotiated. The angry person may be feeling so physically shaken (and/or possibly full of guilt or remorse), from having blown their top that they may be anxious to sweep everything under the carpet as soon as possible. So, the suggestion that you renew the 'contract' between you may have to come from you. Open up discussion on how you can prevent the misunderstanding from occurring again. Say how you are willing to change, or compromise, and ask for anything you may want to see happening differently. You may have to suggest that you meet at a later date to discuss what has happened. This will give the other person a chance to calm down and enable them to present some rational arguments so that you can have some constructive feedback. It will also give you a chance to prepare your 'defence', if that is what you wish to do

- **Acknowledge regret** – Apologize, if appropriate. Tell the other person what you have learned from the experience.

Table 13

Chapter 9

Improving your relationships

Many people take a fatalistic approach to relationships: 'You either get on well with someone or you don't'; 'You're either a "born mother" or you're not'; 'You're either lucky to be able to hit it off with people at work, or you're not.' Many millions of women faithfully read their horoscopes each week in the hope that the stars will guide them in the direction of Mr Right. Nobody, after all, with any romance about them would want to accept that marriage is a relationship which has to be *worked* at, and wouldn't we all like to think that we all had a Mother Earth deep inside us to guide us effortlessly through motherhood!

Michael Argyle, an eminent social psychologist, who has done extensive research into relationships, writes in his book *The Anatomy of Relationships*, (Penguin, 1985):

To some extent there are biological dispositions toward particular kinds of relationships, the mother-child relation is the most instinctive; the need of men and women for a permanent mate may be another innate pattern. More important for the other kinds, is socialisation, whereby we learn the concepts of 'friend', 'love', and the rest, and the rules of proper behaviour in each case . . . people often have difficulty with social situations of various kinds; they can be helped by the discovery of the styles of behaviour that are most effective, and then by training in these skills.

As confident women, we have to review the rules we originally learned about relationships; perhaps they now need updating. If we decide they do, then, as Michael Argyle suggests, we may need to learn to behave differently. The kind of behaviour that he, and other psychologists with experience in this field suggests, is, in effect, the very behaviour this book has been advocating. So here are some general guidelines for most kinds of social relationships.

A confident woman:

- Knows that there is a strong link between good relationships and health and happiness and she wants all three!

- Makes an effort to understand the rules of each relationship

- Is prepared to negotiate changes and modifications to these rules

- Is willing to acquire knowledge (for example, through reading) which may enable her to improve and develop her relationships

- Is prepared, within reason, to alter her behaviour to improve the relationship

- Is prepared to ask the 'other parties' in her relationships to alter their behaviour

- Is prepared to acknowledge when there are problems in a relationship

- Is willing to seek help from a 'third party' to sort out any difficulties if she is unable to manage without assistance

- Is prepared to leave a relationship if she has made a sincere effort to do the above and has been unsuccessful.

Let's now take a closer look at some common relationships of confident women and see what kind of attitudes and behaviour we would expect to find. Check your relationships against the following profiles, and if they are found wanting (and who can claim perfection?), vow to take some action.

The confident friend

- Chooses to spend her precious time with people she really likes and does not waste energy trying to be liked by everybody

- Can choose her friends from all walks of life and all generations and does not need everybody to be like her

- Has realistic expectations of her friends and does not expect them all to meet all of her needs. She can be more serious with some, more loving with some, and have fun with others

- Does not demand that her friends all get on well together. She respects and values their differences

- Knows which of her friends she can turn to for support in times of difficulty, and is, therefore, not hurt or shocked when the 'whole gang' fail to turn up for the rescue operation

- Accepts the right of her friends to say 'no' to her requests. She doesn't experience this as a total rejection of her

- Can defend her own right to say 'no' and be independent and private sometimes. This includes reserving her right not to get involved with her friends' problems on every occasion. She is able to feel secure in the knowledge that she 'does her bit' and is not prepared to come to everyone's rescue during every crisis

- Is able to disagree and give constructive criticism about specific behaviours and attitudes which she observes and does not like

- Is able to withstand losing some friends as she grows and develops and is willing and prepared to make new, and perhaps more appropriate ones.

The confident wife or partner

- Is prepared to take the risk of making a long-term commitment

- Can assertively negotiate a mutually satisfactory partnership. She does not live with the fantasy that everything will work out, given some time and patience. She does not think that this kind of discussion will threaten any romance or 'magic' in the relationship

- Can be satisfied with this relationship even if it is unusual or does not fit in with other people's expectations

- Is able to negotiate financial and other conditions which are just and equitable

- Is able to negotiate domestic arrangements which are mutually satisfactory and which may not be in vogue

- Can be an individual within her own right within the partnership, even during periods in which she may choose to be dependent on her partner (for example, child rearing). She is able to maintain her own values, interests and friends and is able to resist pressure which may be put on her to always 'be a couple'

- Can allow her partner his or her individuality and independence within the mutually agreed boundaries. She is able to object when these boundaries have been crossed, for example, when trust has been broken, or she, or other people such as her children, have been treated unfairly

- She can tolerate some differences in values, attitudes and behaviour, perhaps due to class, race, religion or gender. This includes making an attempt to understand and empathize with some of these differences

- Can assertively give and receive criticism. She is able to see that mutual criticism is essential to any intimate relationship, and enables it to grow and develop

● Is able to get angry, receive anger and accept mutual for-giveness.

The confident lover

● Chooses partners she is attracted to, or wants to be with, and not just ones which she feels she ought to have, or other people think she ought to have. They could be short or tall, young or old, male or female, black or white. She knows that someone's attraction to her does not guarantee that the feeling will be, or ought to be, mutual, so she is able to say 'no' assertively. She doesn't have to resort to lies, half-truths and false promises

● Is in tune with her own body. She accepts it as 'her', in the same way that she accepts her mind, or her soul. She is aware of the signals that it sends out and, therefore, is rarely in the position of being surprised by it. She always feels in control of its needs and wants. She doesn't get into situations where she says afterwards, 'I don't know what came over me,' or 'It (that is, lust) hit me between the eyes and I had no power to resist.'

● Respects and loves her body. She looks after it well, so that she is not ashamed of it. She will not let others degrade or abuse it. She is prepared to ask for protection from any unwanted pregnancy or from disease

● She is not seduced into giving her body away as a 'favour' because she feels sorry for someone, or because they are trying to make her feel guilty for arousing their passion

● She is well-informed. If her sex education was less than perfect as a growing girl, she knows she has a right to important information and is not too embarrassed to obtain it

● She can negotiate the quantity and quality of lovemaking which she and her partner enjoy. She doesn't have to resort to reassurances from magazines, or other people, that their pattern, positions, or her orgasm, are 'normal' or satisfactory

- She can be warm, open, spontaneous, adventurous and passionate, without losing her ultimate control.

The confident mother

- She is happy to be less than perfect. She can admit her mistakes and is prepared to learn from them. She knows that her goal is to provide 'good-enough' mothering and not to achieve sainthood

- She has a sense of her own values, which may differ from her mother's, her neighbour's or any other parents with whom she may be compared

- She is prepared to defend these values within her family, and in the outside world. This may involve arguments and negotiations at home or at school, or in any other situation where they are challenged

- She is aware that, after giving a child a sense of basic security and love, the most important influence on her children's development will be her own attitudes and behaviour. For example, she knows that the way she looks after herself will determine the way her children will tend to look after themselves; she knows that the kind of relationship she has with her partner will influence her childrens' attitudes to relationships in their adult life; she knows that, if she is assertive, her children are more likely to be so; she knows that if she is happy her children are more likely to grow up with the ability to be happy and enjoy life

- If she is a working mother, she will not feel compelled to compete in the Superwoman stakes. She is prepared to ask for help from her partner, her family, her employers and the state to enable her to fulfil these two often conflicting roles satisfactorily. This may mean entrusting some aspects of her parenting role to others

- She does not abuse her power as an adult and is able to help her children develop a sense of their own power gradually. In many day-to-day situations, she encourages shared decision-making, but is able to take full responsibility for her children in situations where she judges that the advice and wisdom of an adult is needed. This may involve disciplining and punishing a child appropriately when she or he has, knowingly, 'broken the rules'

- She encourages her children to develop their independence and is prepared to teach them the skills to achieve this when they have reached the appropriate age. She is also prepared to allow them to take reasonable risks and learn from their own mistakes without resorting to a stream of 'I told you so' retorts

- She allows her children to develop their own sense of values and to act upon them, as long as they are not harming themselves or others

- She does not expect her children to look after her; she is prepared to take responsibility for her own life, with all its sadness and happiness. On the other hand, she can assertively take their help and support if, and when, it is freely given

- She gives mothering without strings attached to it. She does not expect her children to feel everlastingly guilty for the sacrifices she may have chosen to make in order to care for them

- She does not have expectations for her children's adulthood; she allows them to have the lifestyle, career and relationships which they choose. She does not use emotional or financial blackmail to influence them to fulfil her hopes, or indeed, her own unrealized ambitions or fantasies.

The confident employee

- She values her skills and aptitudes and wishes them to be used to their full potential. She is prepared to assert her right to use this potential and will oppose any attempt to strangle it

- She expects job satisfaction and will try to ensure that she is not bored or given the impossible to achieve. She uses her experience to suggest ways in which the job could be made more interesting and effective

- She values her health and welfare and is not prepared to work under conditions which could damage either

- She knows her stress threshold and is prepared to argue her case, so that her workload does not prematurely burn her out

- She expects to have adequate information, training and resources with which to do her job effectively and is prepared to campaign to have more of these made available, if necessary

- She believes in equal opportunities for everyone and is prepared to fight any known injustices

- She will not tolerate sexual or any other kind of harrassment

- She keeps her own flirtatious behaviour strictly within the boundaries of her personal relationships

- She is not prepared to resort to behind-the-back techniques, manipulation or aggression, unless assertive techniques have been tried and the situation remains intolerable

- She is not afraid of, or ashamed of, being successful, but on the other hand is prepared to sacrifice ambition for other rewards, if she so chooses

- She is aware of her limitations and is willing to learn new skills. She welcomes constructive criticism and can protect herself from put-down behaviour

- She is prepared to be managed by others more senior than herself but always retains her right to express disagreement with this management. While negotiating for changes she is prepared to work by the existing rules, unless basic human rights are being seriously abused

- She does not feel threatened by sharing her own knowledge and skills with others

- She maintains good working relationships with her colleagues and is able to work as a member of a team

- She expects her personal life to be treated with respect. This includes maintaining her privacy, if she so wishes, and having support and understanding when she is experiencing stress in her life outside work.

The confident boss

- She enjoys her position of influence, and is proud of the achievements which brought her to this post

- She never uses her power to abuse, exploit, or humiliate others less successful, or less powerful, than herself

- She encourages good communication between all employees and ensures that it flows openly up, down and across all organizational levels. She sets an example by not hiding in an ivory tower

- She encourages and rewards assertive behaviour and welcomes constructive criticism and innovatory ideas. This may mean having to consider changes in the organizational structure

- She can make decisions but does so after seeking the opinions and feelings of other knowledgeable and interested parties

- She is prepared to admit mistakes and shortcomings and is prepared to learn from them. She does not need to sit on a pedestal to support her own self-esteem

- She wishes to continue to improve the skills and knowledge of everyone in the organization, including herself

- She does not feel threatened and anxious if people are having fun at work as well as doing a good job

- She is able to criticize and discipline people who are not abiding by the rules of the organization, or fulfilling their contract.

The confident client, customer or patient

- She expects a satisfactory service and is prepared to complain if this is not received. She is not prepared to pay full price for second best, neither does she expect a lesser service if she is entitled to have it free, or at a reduced rate

- She asks for full information on the product or service she

is seeking or receiving. She will not be 'fobbed off' with
technical jargon used to mystify and de-power her

- She always reserves the right to question the price and ask
  for justification of the cost. She equally has a right to ask
  for a reduction if she considers the price to be over-inflated

- She expects to be treated with courtesy and respect and will
  object at being treated in any other manner

- She exposes any hint of sexism, or any other kind of unjust
  practice

- She always reserves her right to obtain a second opinion
  or another estimate

- She is able to make an initial enquiry, without knowing
  exactly what it is she is wanting, and is able to withstand
  any pressure to buy before she is ready

- She is aware that she has rights as a consumer, and is
  prepared to fight for these rights. She will always use her

assertive skills first, but reserves the right to consider other means to make an injustice known and corrected

- She is prepared to take her custom elsewhere and does not always need to justify such a decision.

Chapter 10

Planning your programme for change

By now, hopefully, you have a clear idea of what confidence is all about and are convinced that you would like to change some of your own attitudes and behaviour. Your next step is to set yourself a realistic programme for change. This section has been designed to give you a basic structure to use. It contains a series of exercises and games which you can use either on your own or in a self-help group. If you work through these exercises, in sequence, you will have completed a basic programme in confidence-building, based on the theory and principles which I have discussed in the first two sections. At the end of the programme on page 185, you will find an evaluation sheet. If you complete this, you will be able to assess your progress and make plans for doing further work on any areas which still need developing. Chapters 12 and 13 will guide you in the direction which you have chosen to take.

General guidelines

Be patient

We cannot change the habits of a lifetime overnight. Slow, steady progress is what we should aim for, not instant miracle cures. Don't be tempted to skip the first sections of your programme, because they are the foundations upon which the second half will be built.

Remember the golden rule of learning theory is that we

must always start with the small problems. We must choose, at first, to work where there is least risk, otherwise our anxiety will be too great and we will once again experience failure. We must patiently build on our small successes piece by piece. For example, don't start by trying to assert yourself at work if it means that you may lose your job, or don't start at home, if it may mean that you will lose your partner. When you have become generally more confident you may well decide that both are dispensable. Practise changing your behaviour in situations which are relatively neutral for you. For everyone these situations will be different, but they often include relating to people on a more superficial level, such as in a bus queue, on the beach, in shops, on holiday or at conferences and meetings. On the other hand, if you feel relatively secure at home or at work, these may be the places for you to start.

Be persistent

There will be times when the road feels very long and your path full of immovable obstacles. Perhaps these feelings indicate that you have temporarily exhausted yourself, so have a rest and look back at your progress so far. Allow yourself time to recover and consolidate what you have already learned. If you are working on your own, this may be the time to get some support; if you are working with a group, share your feelings.

Enjoy yourself

Remember that we learn best when we are relatively relaxed. We need enough adrenalin in our blood to keep us alert and interested but we certainly do not need to be in a state of frozen terror! This kind of self-development work should not feel heavy and onerous; even if it is occasionally a little painful, it should be stimulating and interesting for most of the time. Check that you are giving yourself plenty of treats and rewards.

Don't compare yourself with others

Even if you are working in a group, try to remember that everyone is different and that the progress of each individual will depend on an infinite number of variables. The only evaluation of your progress which is worth having is one which is based on the comparison of your present attitudes and behaviour with those which you started out with. These should be considered in the context of your very own present, personal situation and your background.

Don't allow others to judge your progress

Only you can be the ultimate judge of your own behaviour and feelings. Don't be tempted to seek constant reassurance from others about your progress. Yes, you want support, encouragement and constructive feedback, but not judgement. The only judgement you must allow is from people, such as employers, who may demand a confident style of behaviour as part of their contract with you.

Don't forget that your ultimate aim is to feel confident and not just to appear confident. Only you can feel your feelings, even though you may have many 'amateur psychologists' in your life who think they know you better than you!

Working on your own

Working on your own is difficult, but you may have to do the programme this way because you have no alternative. On the other hand, you may decide that this is how you would prefer to tackle it. The following guidelines should be helpful:

- **Separate your two roles** – Whatever the reason, you will have to remember that you have two roles to play: that of teacher or counsellor and that of pupil or client. Sometimes these roles come into conflict and all progress is halted while the fight ensues. For example, as a frustrated teacher you may want to kick and bully yourself into action; as a disillusioned and weary pupil you may want to rebel and play hooky!

  As your teacher or counsellor, you can do the preparatory work and organization and then leave your 'pupil/client' to do their 'homework' on their own. Your 'teacher/counsellor' can then return when the task is completed and evaluate, encourage and reward

- **Get yourself a special file** – This is for your personal development work. Find somewhere private to keep it. This can be used to keep your work in and to file away any interesting cuttings from newspapers, etc. You can also jot down notes at any time during the week and then pop them in the file to think about later

- **Find somewhere quiet and relaxing to work** – Somewhere you will not be disturbed by callers or by the telephone

- **Set aside a regular time** – Set aside perhaps one evening per week if possible, to work on your programme. Two hours of this time can be spent on doing games and exercises. Allow yourself a break of about 20 minutes in between the hours. This can be a time for treating yourself to a drink and favourite 'goodie' to eat. This is a time which is precious, so make sure it is not used for anything else. It may help to do an 'attendance register' for yourself which you could pin up in a prominent place. You could list the dates you have set aside for your programme and tick them when you have completed your work. You will soon get an idea whether or not you are giving your programme the priority it deserves

- **Set yourself some realistic goals** – A reasonable goal for someone who had a full-time job plus several other commitments would, I suggest, be one session a week. During any one session you may complete between two and five exercises, so you would expect to have completed this programme in about four months. For anyone to complete it in less than two months would probably be unrealistic because, if the exercises are to be effective, there must be enough time to integrate your learning into real-life situations

- **Keep dated notes and comments** – Keep notes on your work in your file. You may want to note, for example, if you feel you need further practice in a certain area or would like to do some reading on a particular subject. You can refer to these when you complete your final evaluation

- **Ask for support and feedback** – The importance of this has been discussed several times but it cannot be too heavily emphasized. But don't forget to choose the people you ask with care.

Working in a self-help group

This way of working would be my first choice because you have the built-in support of people who understand and care about what you are trying to do. Many people are frightened of groups, and I can understand that it is difficult sometimes to imagine yourself opening up to other people but I have now seen many hundreds of people successfully overcome this initial fear and become positively hooked on the fun and excitement you can have when working in this way! The following guidelines should help you, if you have never set up a group before:

- **Size of the group** – Your group does not have to be very large; you could certainly do some very useful work with four people. A small group is often easier to organize in terms of getting people together at the same time and also you do not require large premises. A larger group has the advantage of allowing you to practise with a variety of different people and perhaps make some new friends. For this kind of work, I would suggest that an ideal size is about eight people and that twelve should be the maximum number

- **Members** – The wider the range of people you can have, the more interesting your group will be. So, try to have people of all ages and people from a variety of social backgrounds. Your local Council for Voluntary Service will advise you on how to form a group, obtain premises, etc.

  If you decide that you want to work with a group of friends, you must be careful to respect confidences exchanged within the group. You should also be careful to choose friends who you think will be able to give you constructive, honest, feedback. Remember that doing this kind of work together can either make or break a friendship. I know that I have many friends with whom I would not choose to be in a group; I value my relationship with them for other reasons.

Keep the same membership, if possible, throughout the programme because then you will have built up some trust in each other by the time you move on to some of the more testing exercises, such as giving and taking criticism

- **Leadership** – Always be clear about who is the leader for each session. You are not necessarily looking for a budding therapist, or a grand charismatic character, but someone who can, simply, give some structure to the session, because it is so easy to go off course or allow certain people to dominate. This kind of programme is ideal for rotating leadership. The group needs someone to take responsibility for: starting the session – on time! – organizing materials such as pen, paper and coffee; reminding the group of their task, if they were off track; suggesting a 'homework' task; closing the group – on time!

  Taking this role can be a confidence-building exercise in itself.

- **Structure** – Agree to meet for a certain number of sessions initially and then review your progress, as individuals and as a group, at least every two months. Initially, meetings at weekly intervals are ideal because there is enough time to try out your new behaviour and attitudes but not enough time to forget that you have embarked on this course! After your first eight weeks you could start meeting at fortnightly intervals, as you should all have acquired the habit of doing your 'homework'.

  Do not plan too long a session; this kind of work can be exhausting. Two hours with a break halfway through is a comfortable length of time

- **'Warm-ups'** – it often helps to start the group with some kind of ritual, game or exercise to help bring you all together and to enable everyone to feel involved. For example, this may be quite simply each of you sharing your progress since the last session. Alternatively, you could play a fun 'ice-breaker' game. There are plenty of books now available which include a wide variety of such games and they are listed on page 189. These games can be very useful for helping a group to 'gel' together and feel less inhibited with each other. It is my experience, though, that they can have the reverse effect in groups where people are feeling very shy and anxious. So, perhaps it may be wise to play safe at the start of your group and then as you get to know each other, you can be a little more adventurous with the warm-ups you use

- **Games and exercises** – Remember that even some of the most simple-looking exercises can unexpectedly bring up strong feelings for people, so always allow plenty of time for sharing these feelings and for general discussion. Never be tempted to move on to the next exercise just because you had planned to complete a certain number of exercises during that session. Always move at a mutually agreed, comfortable pace for the group. You may choose to spend a whole session just talking and sharing sometimes. Your support for each others' struggle to be confident in the real world is just as important as completing any of the exercises

- **Role-play** – Many people find the idea of doing role-plays terrifying and this is why I do not tend to introduce them until at least halfway through a course. By this time your confidence has already been enhanced and you trust the group enough to not mind looking silly so much. No one should ever be cajoled into doing this kind of work before they are ready; if anxiety levels are too high, the stage is set for failure. It is always useful to have one or two people playing the role of observers, so they can give feedback to the participants in the role-plays. Anyone who is especially nervous can be given this role and will still learn an immense amount from just watching

- **Ending sessions** – Finish with a ritual or game which will involve everyone and which will also take your attention outside the group again. For example, you could each share one of your homework goals for the week

- **Have fun** – This kind of work can sometimes feel heavy and depressing, so build some light relief into your programme. These could be fun games or just going out together for a drink. You will all feel much more committed to completing the programme if you are enjoying yourselves

- **Be creative** – Make up your own games and exercises to supplement the programme and if they work well, please send me the details!

1) PATIENCE.
2) PERSISTENCE.
3) FUN.
4) FEEDBACK.
5) EVALUATION

IN

1) COMPARISONS.
2) BULLYING YOURSELF.
3) DESTRUCTIVE CRITICISM.
4) LONG SESSIONS.
5) UNREALISTIC GOALS.

OUT

Chapter 11

Practical exercises

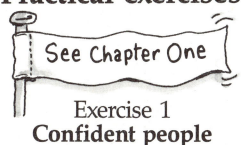

See Chapter One

Exercise 1
Confident people

Individuals

Over a period of a week or so, make a list of all the confident people you can think of, including people you know personally, and people who are publicly well-known, for example, through their appearances on TV or other forms of media.

Beside the name of each person, jot down three qualities (such as, honesty, determination, courage, etc.) which you admire in them.

From your list, select the six qualities which you consider to be most important.

Tick the qualities which you already possess (even though they may be very latent!) and select one from the others, which you would like to possess or expand.

During the next week, think about this particular quality, talk to other people about it, observe it in other people and ask yourself what advantages they have from possessing it (for example, her courage enabled her to apply for that job; to tell the manager that the targets were unrealistic; to tell her mother that she wouldn't be spending Christmas at home; to wear bright red nail polish; to join a dating agency, etc.).

You should also note how you could change your life if you possessed, or extended, this quality in yourself.

Groups

Everyone should sit, or lie, comfortably, with eyes closed and you should put on some relaxing music for five minutes or so. Think of a confident person whom you admire. Imagine how they spend their days at work, at home, on their holidays, and so on.

Imagine that each of you are those people you were thinking about, and get up and move around the room. Introduce yourselves to as many people as possible; ask each other questions.

After ten minutes or so, divide into pairs and each take turns to share what it felt like to be that person.

Together share the kind of thoughts and ideas suggested in the exercise for individuals.

See Chapter One

Exercise 2
The devil's advocate

Individuals

Spend a few minutes thinking about people you know, who might think you a little 'odd' or self-indulgent for buying and reading this book. This is the last kind of book you would imagine that they would have on their coffee table, not necessarily because they are confident themselves, but rather because they would consider this kind of 'therapy stuff' at its best, unnecessary, and at its worst, positively dangerous. (They would think it would make people too selfish and self-conscious.)

Try to feel yourself 'into their shoes' and write a letter to yourself, warning you against the dangers of getting involved in this kind of activity and perhaps giving you some other advice about how to sort your problems out (for example, pulling yourself together; getting down to some hard work or thinking of others worse off than yourself!).

Write another imaginary letter from the real you in reply to this letter, defending your beliefs about your right to change and to use these methods to help you.

Groups

Divide into two groups and each take a large piece of paper and some felt tips. The first group should do a brainstorm on the arguments against doing confidence-building courses such as this, and the second one on the arguments in favour.

After 10 to 15 minutes re-assemble the large group and proceed to have a debate, or a not-so-polite slanging match, if you are feeling lively! It is a good idea to start by giving each group two or three minutes to put over their case, in the first instance, without interruptions and heckles.

This exercise is usually good fun and can help break the ice for a new, and perhaps rather anxious, group.

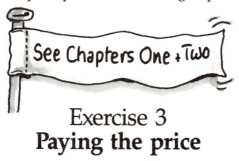

See Chapters One + Two

Exercise 3
Paying the price

Individuals

Using this list as a guide, note down the price you are paying, or have paid, for not being as confident as you would like.

- **At work** – For example, 'I'm bored'; 'I'm intimidated'; 'I don't put across my point very well at meetings'; 'I'm under-achieving'.

- **Educational opportunities/career choice** – 'I should have had better "A" level grades'; or 'I drifted into this career'.

- **Friends** – 'I haven't enough'; 'I always end up doing what they want to do.'

- **My love life** – 'I am not getting what I need and want'; 'I find it difficult to say 'no', so I am getting resentful'; 'I am stuck in a relationship which I don't enjoy'.

Continue this exercise looking at other relationships and areas of your life, such as children; parents, in-laws or other family; social life; holidays.

Note down the price your body is paying, or is likely to pay, for example, headaches; stomach upsets; chronic tension; over or under-eating. Also note the price your appearance is paying, such as, if you are overweight, dowdy or don't spend much money on clothes.

Groups

Do the above exercise in pairs and then each of you take it in turn to summarize, to the rest of the group, the price your partner is paying. It's very salutory to hear this public announcement and can increase our resolve to change!

See Chapter One

Exercise 4
The world we live in

Individuals

Over a period of a week, make a list, of all the facets in our society (including its sexism), which you feel may contribute towards people not being very confident. Use Newspapers, TV, books and discussions with other people to help you.

Make a large collage of photos, cuttings, and so on, to make up a composite picture of the world which is partly responsible for your difficulties. Look at this picture, or try to recall it whenever you are feeling besieged with guilt!

Groups

Choose a number of facets of society you would like to discuss, for example, gender issues, the educational system, politics, the economic system, the media. Divide into small groups and each use a large sheet of paper on which to brainstorm your ideas. (Brainstorming means that people can say whatever comes into their head, without having to justify it and it is added to the sheet. It is an excellent way of using the creative energy and thinking process of a group.) You can share and discuss each sheet with the rest of the group.

Exercise 5
Personal histories

Individuals

Reread the list of possible influences on pages 20-21 and make a note of as many factors as you can remember. For example:

● My mum was always comparing me to my sister

● My parents were unhappy and my Mum said she only stayed at home because she had no choice

● My Dad didn't have any patience with me

● I was the youngest and nobody could be bothered to teach me anything

● I was laughed at at school because I wore glasses

● We were poor (or too rich!), etc.

Note down the kind of changes you would have asked a Fairy Godmother to make and think whether or not these would have made any difference to your problems of confidence.

Give yourself some kind of comforting treat, which will symbolize your new, and more understanding and caring, attitude towards yourself.

Groups

Each person should do the first two parts of the above exercise on their own, and then divide into pairs or small groups and share your histories with each other.

Place two chairs or cushions opposite each other; and each person takes it in turn to sit opposite the empty chair or cushion and address it as though it was an offending parent/teacher/institution/friend. Start by completing the sentence: 'You damaged my self-confidence when . . .' You could say, for example, 'by being so over-protective of me'; 'by being so violent'; 'by telling me that all men were rotten'; 'that I would never get to university'; 'by not standing up to my father . . .'

It is important to remember that this is not intended to be a rehearsal for anything you might say in real life; it is just therapy for you; it helps you to clear away some of the unexpressed feelings, such as resentment, which may be blocking you from moving forward.

See Chapter One

Exercise 6
Sex roles

Individuals

Using the table on page 27, note the items on both lists which you feel describe your behaviour.

Show the table to a friend and ask them to use the list to comment on your behaviour, as they see it, and to note any differences which there may be with your own analysis.

Note whether these stereotypes, or any other messages you have in your head about gender role, have, or still are, affecting your ability to behave with confidence.

During the next week make a list of women who you consider to be both confident and feminine, and closely observe their behaviour.

Groups

Do the above exercise in pairs or a small group.

Each of you should choose one item off the list which you would like to develop in your own personality, and each should give a two minute talk to the rest of the group on why you have made that choice. For example, you might say:

I want to become more analytical because I have developed an awful habit of rushing too quickly into things. My father always said I was headstrong and daft as a brush; it seems that I am hell-bent on proving him right! I think that I'm often putting on an act of knowing exactly what I want to do, but underneath, I haven't a clue. I'm so frightened that if I stop to think, it will all seem too complex or frightening and I'll never do anything . . . I would like you to let me know when you see me behaving in this way and praise me when you notice that I am being analytical.

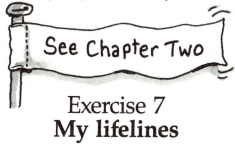

See Chapter Two

Exercise 7
My lifelines

Individuals

Make a list of all your friends, family and acquaintances with whom you are in regular contact.

Tick the ones who you think will positively encourage you to change your behaviour and life. Put a cross beside the ones who are likely to try and sabotage the process by disparaging remarks, getting uptight when you begin to assert yourself with them, and so on.

Make a list of the ways in which you think you would like to receive your support and help, and beside each enter the names of the friends, etc., who might be able to give you this. For example:

- 'Booster' chats on the phone: Jean

- Honest feedback on my behaviour: Adrian and Maggie

- Condolences when the road is sticky: Jean

- Help with role-plays and exercises: Adrian, Maggie, and Laura

- Praise and rewards when you achieve: Adrian and Jean.

Speak to each of these people and tell them that you are doing a confidence-building programme and would like their help in the above specific areas. Make the necessary arrangements and then reward yourself for having the confidence to ask for what you need!

Groups

Each person should spend two minutes with every person in the group asking for specific help during the course. Explain why you need this help. Everyone reserves the right to say they cannot give the help requested, and to perhaps say what they are prepared to do. Keep notes if you feel you are likely to forget or become confused with the different requests. For example:

- Joan: ring each Thursday

- Angela: give feedback when I hear her putting herself down

- Pauline: check that she is using 'I' statements

- Jane: let her know when I see her interrupting anyone

- Brenda: give her genuine compliments.

See Chapter Four

Exercise 8
Rewards

Individuals

Following the guide on pages 62-3, make a list of rewards which you can use to help you on this programme. Pin it up in a prominent place in your home and each time you use one put a tick beside it. Check the list each Saturday to see how often you are rewarding yourself; try to increase the ticks and move further down your list each week. Change the list if the rewards become stale or your tastes change!

Groups

Each person should make a list of their rewards and read it out to the rest of the group. This exercise is invariably very enlightening when it is done with other people. It is a very safe way of beginning to share personal information, but it also affirms each person's individuality, because we usually learn that what is one person's idea of a reward is another person's idea of a punishment!

The pooling of ideas is also very useful and often one or two people will have found the exercise very difficult. The group can then give support and help these people understand the reasons for their difficulty.

See Chapter Two

Exercise 9
Fantasy of the future

Individuals

Choose a quiet place where you can be on your own for an hour or so. First put on some gentle music and sit or lie in a relaxed position with your eyes closed for five minutes. Allow yourself slowly to begin to fantasize about your life in five years' time. Imagine that you have become as self-confident as you wish to be, and picture your day-to-day life. When you feel ready, begin to write a letter to a real or imaginary friend (that is, as the 'new you'). This is a friend who you have not seen for very many years and you are inviting them to come and stay. In the letter you describe your life, your work, your home life and also try to describe the changes she or he might notice in your behaviour from the time when they knew you several years ago. You may even like to give yourself a new name.

Groups

Follow the first half of the above instructions but instead of writing the letter, break into small groups and introduce yourself, as the 'you' who you had been imagining you might be in five years' time. Ask each other questions, about their life such as, 'How did you find such a good job?', 'How did you meet your friend?'; 'What are you wearing?'; 'Where are you living?'; 'How did you spend last week-end?'

Super Confidence

See Chapter Three

Exercise 10
'I am'

Individuals

This is a favourite exercise of mine. It sounds so simple but is often very difficult to do, and each time I do it, I learn something new about myself or I become aware of how much I've changed since the last time I did it.

Complete the sentence 'I am . . .', as many times as you can, without thinking hard and just putting down whatever comes into your head, without censoring it. Cover two or three sides of paper with the sentences before stopping.

Re-read the list, slowly and out loud. Tick the sentences which you feel comfortable with and mark with a cross or red pen those with which you are not happy.

Review the list and consider whether or not you would feel comfortable showing it to anyone. Think who might agree with your list and who might not. Note down the main discrepancies. For example, you may have written 'I am selfish' and perhaps very few people might agree with you; or perhaps you might have written 'I am shy' but maybe some people would be surprised to read that. If you can, show it to a couple of friends and discuss it.

Groups

Do the above exercise and, in pairs or small groups, read out your lists to each other. Discuss any difficulties or surprises you may have had. If you have only recently met, this exercise will help you to realize what kind of first impression you have made on each other. Have you given a true and correct picture of the kind of people you are, or have you kept your lights under bushels and your skeletons in the cupboards?

Practical exercises

See Chapter Three

Exercise 11
Strengths and weaknesses

Individuals

Make a list of your weaknesses, as both you and other people perceive them. When you have completed the list try to find the positive side of each of these characteristics or 'failings'.

For example:

- Untidy
- Shy
- Quiet
- A worrier

- Not obsessional
- Modest
- Not loud and boisterous
- Think carefully

Can you, or do you want to, own any of the positive qualities?

Now make a list of your strengths, perhaps using the above list to help you. Mark with a red pen those strengths which you will need, or could use, to help you achieve your goals (which will include becoming more confident, of course!)

Pin this list up in a prominent place in your house, so that you and others can see and read it daily. Add to it as you remember additional strengths and as you acquire new skills. No one in your house has to feel left out in this game because they too can put their list up!

Groups

Do the first part of this exercise on your own and then break into pairs and share your lists. Note down each others' weaknesses and keep the list for future reference. Make a contract with each other to note when your partner is putting themselves down about their weaknesses and remind them of the positive aspects or of one of their other strengths. At the end of the course, look at the lists again and give each other feedback on how you think you have progressed. Share any strengths you may have observed in each other and add these to your original lists.

See Chapter Three

Exercise 12
Self-advertisement

Individuals

Imagine that you are a brilliant copywriter for an advertising agency and the product you have been asked to market is the real you! Draft some advertising material for a) an advert for a newspaper's personal column and b) a letter to a firm who may be interested in employing you. Remember that there are strict codes of ethics in this advertising agency and only the truth must be told. The art will be in presenting this truth in its most positive light. Draw a rough design for a logo for yourself and think of any additional materials you might like to use, such as photos, certificates, quotes from references or friends.

Show your work to a friend for comment and embellishment!

Groups

Each person should write an 'advertisement' for themselves, using information on their personality rather than appearance or role in society. Without writing your names on these adverts, you should place them all in a large container. Give them a shake and pass the container around. Each person should take an advert out. If they find their own, they should replace it and take an alternative. Take it in turns to read the adverts and guess which belongs to whom.

Discuss together how you felt about doing this exercise. Was it difficult, perhaps, to leave out details about your job or your appearance, or did that make it easier?

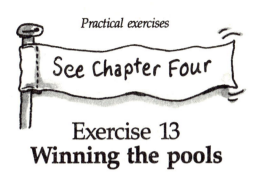

Practical exercises

See Chapter Four

Exercise 13
Winning the pools

Individuals

Imagine that you have won £25,000 on the pools. You have been told that you can only have this money if it is spent within one month. £5,000 must be spent on yourself and the other £20,000 is to be spent on other people. No money must be saved or given away as cash. Be completely honest and do what you *want* to do with the money, rather than what you think you *ought* to do.

Plan, immediately, without thinking too much, how you would spend this money and make some notes. Return to this plan several days later, after talking it through with friends and see whether you feel compelled to alter it in any way. If so, consider why you have made these alterations. Have your plans been affected by other people's values or are you changing your own values for some reason?

Groups

Do the above exercise in pairs and each person tells the rest of the group how their partner is going to spend the money.

Discuss how you all felt about hearing your 'values' publicly exposed and whether or not you were affected by other people's opinions and values.

A useful extension to this exercise is to imagine how your mother and father, or any other significant people in your life, would have spent this money and to reflect on the similarities and differences.

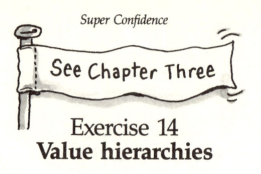

See Chapter Three

Exercise 14
Value hierarchies

Individuals

Make a list of your ten most important values (such as being kind, honest, courageous, just, etc.). Place them in a hierarchical order, with the most important at the head of the list. Ask yourself if the list contains any values which:

- You would give up a job for.

- You would lose a friendship over.

- You would be prepared to die for. If so, in what circumstances?

- You might kill to defend.

Note which values you are experiencing difficulties in living up to and ask yourself whether you have unrealistic expectations of yourself. Are you trying to be perfect or trying to live up to impossible values set, perhaps, by other people?

If you decide these are values which you do want to live up to, select one each week to focus on. Pay special attention to this value all week, initiate discussion about it, notice when it is being respected, or not respected by other people, list the names of people who you think live their lives respecting this value, note how they cope with the problems you encounter. Could you cope in a similar way?

When you have worked your way through the list, see whether you need to rearrange the hierarchy and note what changes you need to make in your behaviour and lifestyle order to live comfortably with your values.

Groups

Brainstorm a number of values which your group considers important. Taking each value in turn, imagine that you have a long line going from one end of the room to the other. One end of this line represents the extreme position people might take to defend this value (such as, to die for it) and the other: the position people might take if they were not prepared to risk anything to defend this value. Members of the group should then place themselves on this line, in a position which represents how they feel about this particular value.

Discuss the exercise in pairs, noting the feelings you experienced and any interesting observations you made about other people's values. This exercise usually brings some surprises!

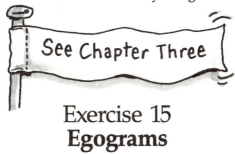

See Chapter Three

Exercise 15
Egograms

Individuals

Using the Transactional Analysis model, this exercise will help you to analyse the relationship between the different parts of your personality. (See Chapter 3, page 51.) Complete the first part, by following the instructions on Table 14.

When you have totalled your scores, make a diagram such as the one below which will show you the parts of your personality in relation to each other. This kind of diagram is called an egogram.

Now examine the egogram and check whether you are happy with the relative proportions of each part. For example, you may note that your Critical Parent (CP) is overshadowing the other parts. If you happen to be in a job which tends to demand you to be authoritative and judgemental (e.g. police force; teaching), you may be satisfied with this relationship, but if you feel that the major roles you have in life do not ask for this kind of behaviour, then you may want to change. Similarly, an actress or painter may be happy with a highly developed Free Child (FC) but an investment consultant might be in danger of losing her job if she had the same kind of egogram. So remember,

Put a tick mark against any of the words, gestures, tones of voice, etc. listed below that you feel you identify with. Make your decisions quickly; do not spend too much time deciding. Total the number of tick marks in each of the vertical columns.

	1	2	3	4	5
Words and phrases	should	good	correct	fun	please
	had	support	how	wow	adapt
	ought	protect	who	want	wish
	always	splendid	why	scared	hope
	insist	care	results	magic	try
	demand	let me	data	natural	if only
	can't	help	alternative	ouch	rebel
	good	don't worry	practical	hi	manipulate
	ridiculous	teach	test	spontaneous	comply
	control	watch	decide	creative	thank you
	good	relax	options	love	obey
Tones of voice	stern	encouraging	confident	free	appealing
	harsh	caring	clear	loud	placating
	commanding	concerned	calm	excited	protesting
	judgemental	supportive	enquiring	chuckling	whining
	critical	sympathetic	even	energetic	submissive
Gestures and postures	points finger	open arms	thoughtful	uninhibited	pouting
	frowns	smiling	alert	loose	helpless
	angry	accepting	listening	bright eyed	sad
	rigid	nodding	erect	exaggerated	dejected
Total =					

Table 14

there are no intrinsically 'good' or 'bad' egograms; you have to decide whether the balance is right for your values and your lifestyle.

If you have noticed that there is one part of your personality which you would like to develop, now is the time to start setting yourself some realistic goals. For example, if you wish to build up your Adult, you could set yourself the task of enrolling on some educational course or watching more documentaries on TV. If you wished to develop your Free Child, you may take up painting or join a drama group. If you wished to develop

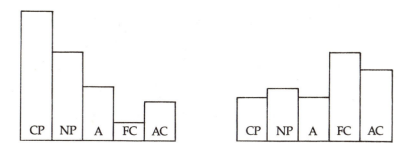

your Nurturing Parent, you could decide to do some voluntary work or start taking better care of yourself!

Remember that this egogram can only be a rough guide and can only indicate the state of current play within your personality. Each time I do this exercise, the result is different. Sometimes it feels as though I am making healthy progress with my personal development and, at other times, I can see that I have begun to let old habits get the upper hand. Unlearning the patterns of childhood behaviour is a long struggle, and when we are under pressure it is easy to slip backwards, so use this exercise from time to time to check your progress.

Groups

Do the first part of the above exercise by completing your egogram. Divide into pairs, and each partner completes what I call a 'guessogram' for the other person. This means you guess how your partner's egogram might look.

Exchange your 'guessograms' and compare with your own; discuss the differences and your feeling in relation to how your personality has been perceived by your partner. Even if you have only known each other a short while this can be a very enlightening exercise; it is always useful to have feedback on the first impressions we create, even if it is of the kind which we would prefer not to hear!

As a group, have some fun doing some 'guessograms' of famous people. One person does a 'guessogram' of a famous person and the rest of the group have to guess who they were thinking of. This will help you to remember the theory but it will also help you to understand each other better, as you share your perceptions and prejudices!

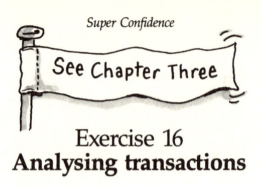

See Chapter Three

Exercise 16
Analysing transactions

Individuals

Watch a TV play or one session of a 'soap'; and, using diagrams such as those in Tables 3 and 4 on pages 52-4, try to keep track of some of the interactions between the characters. Note which are complementary and which are crossed. If you have a video, this exercise will be a lot easier, as you can keep on replaying the scene.

Groups

Six people from the group should volunteer to play being a member of an imaginary committee whose task it is to decide how to spend a certain sum of money. Give each person a role to play, which corresponds to a particular part of the personality, such as Critical Parent, Adapted Child, and so on. Give them a copy of Table 2 to guide them in their behaviour.

The rest of the group should decide how long the committee have in order to make their decision (10 minutes is usually about right). As they speak and interact, note down your observations, such as who becomes the leader; who agrees with whom; which ones are antagonistic to each other; who is finding it difficult to stay in role.

When the laughter has died down, discuss the exercise! Each person shares their impressions and how they identified, or not, with the various characters.

Divide into pairs and discuss how you can use the awareness you may have gained from this exercise.

Exercise 17
My life script

Individuals

Make notes on the outline for the plots of two imaginary stories of your life which significant people, such as your parents, may have written.

Ask yourself how these stories match up to reality. If there are immense differences, why? If there are similarities, are you happy with them? If you would like a different ending to the story, what would it be?

Groups

Spend five minutes relaxing and imagining that one, or both, of your parents are attending a cocktail party which one of your old headteachers is holding for the parents after they have listened to a talk by the local careers officer. Children have not been invited! Picture them talking to other parents about their hopes, expectations and worries about you.

Now imagine that you are one of your parents (or parent figures) and that you are present at that party. Move about the room and talk to as many other 'parents' as you can, about your child (that is, you, as a child!).

Divide into pairs to discuss the feelings engendered by this exercise. Share whether you feel you have been a credit or a disappointment to your parents and whether their opinion of your life still affects your feelings and/or the decisions you may make.

See Chapter Three

Exercise 18
My lifestyle

Individuals

Draw a large circle in the centre of a page and make a pie-chart diagram which will roughly indicate how you allocate your time to various activities. The example below is only a guideline; you will have to choose your own categories.

Time

Draw another circle and complete the same exercise to indicate how you allocate your time with regard to your personal relationships.

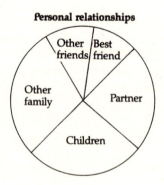

Personal relationships

Draw two more diagrams to indicate how you would like such a chart to look in a year's time.

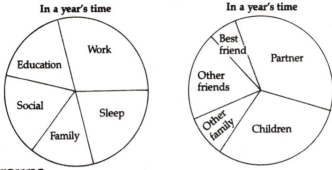

In a year's time   **In a year's time**

Groups

Do the above exercise and then share in pairs. Set each other a realistic goal and agree a time limit and the date on which you will check up on each other's progress.

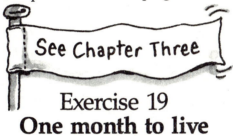

See Chapter Three

Exercise 19
One month to live

Individuals

Imagine that you have been given one month to live. Your health should only fail badly during the last few days but it is possible that your time may be even more restricted. Jot down, in random order, everything you would like to do during this time. Then jot down all the people you would like to say goodbye to.

Reorganize these lists in order of priority.

Prepare a programme for yourself based honestly on meeting your needs and wants, rather than giving any consideration for what you ought to do.

Write a short obituary for yourself.

Write your epitaph.

Look at how your 'programme' may differ from your life now and consider whether you are getting your priorities right today. Are you happy with your obituary and epitaph, will you be remembered in the way you would like to be?

If there are changes you would like to make in your life, set yourself some goals for the next month, which may include doing some of the activities planned in your programme.

Groups

Take it in turns to play interviewer and interviewee. In front of the rest of the group, each person should be interviewed, on the question 'If you only had one month to live what would you do?' Ask each other how you would choose to pass your time; who would you prefer to be with you?

Break into pairs and share the experience of this exercise.

Set each other some goals for the next month. These should include doing at least one of the activities (such as talking to someone about how much you have appreciated knowing them; a visit to somewhere you love) which you have talked about in the interview.

See Chapters Three + Four

Exercise 20
Boasting

Individuals

Write down the answers to the following questions:

- Which parts of my body do I like?

- What aspects of my personality do I like?

- What are some of the things other people have said that they appreciate about me?

- What is my potential? List some of the things you could achieve if you had adequate support and self-confidence.

Sitting in a comfortable and relaxed position, read this list aloud, several times.

Read the list while speaking into a tape-recorder. Replay and note any hesitancies in your voice and the use of any unnecessary qualifiers, such as 'quite', 'fairly' or 'sometimes'.

Ask a friend to listen to you reading your list and to give their comments.

Groups

Each person should complete the first part of the above exercise on their own.

Break into small groups and read your lists to each other. Stop the person reading if you spot any unnecessary qualifiers. Give each other any appreciations which may not have been included on the lists.

Return to the large group and each person should then choose one thing off their list to share with everyone.

See Chapter Five

Exercise 21
Appropriate behaviour

Individuals

Read the tables on pages 71-5. Make a list of a number of situations in which you would choose to use aggressive, passive or assertive behaviour. Try to make each as specific as possible. For example:

- **Aggressive** – Defending my children (or any other 'weak' person) if they were attacked; self-defence; political action against a fascist, repressive regime; telling people if the office caught fire, and no one believed me

- **Passive** – Listening to Aunt Maud (who is very elderly and sick); agreeing, temporarily, to abide by some silly, unnecessary rules at work; running away when being chased by a mugger; having an occasional well-earned rest from being assertive!

- **Assertive** – Asking my colleague to pull her weight at work; ensuring my children are being fairly treated at school; asking my family to help in the house; returning sub-standard goods to a shop.

Think back over the past three weeks and try to recall examples of all three behaviours which you have observed being used by other people (if your memory fails you, watch TV for an hour and do the same!). Make a list of all the non-verbal aspects of the behaviour you noted, putting a tick or a cross beside them, according to whether you judged them appropriate or not. For example:

- Pointing finger (bullies) ✓
- Shifting eyes (interviewee) X
- Weak, drawling voice (politician giving speech) X
- Biting finger nails (staff meeting) X
- Relaxed posture (making a complaint in a hotel) ✓
- Serious expression (correcting children's behaviour) ✓

Groups

Divide into three small groups. Take some large sheets of paper and felt tips. Each group should brainstorm ideas about one of the three kinds of behaviour. Give yourselves the permission to be as prejudiced as you like and note down as many examples of different aspects of the behaviour used by people whom one would generally think of as being either aggressive, passive or assertive. Think about the words they use, their gestures, their usual tone of voice, their jobs, their lifestyles, etc.

In the large group, share these brainstorms and generally discuss and share.

Break into pairs. Each person should spend some time sharing their own habits of using these behaviours inappropriately. Decide which particular one you would like the group to help you with over the next few weeks.

Return to the large group. Each person should say what behaviour their partner would like help with. For example: 'Mary would like you to remind her when she is speaking too quietly'; 'Gill would like you to tell her when you see her scratching her head'; or 'Jane would like to be told when she thumps her fist.'

See Chapter Six

Exercise 22
Assertive rights

Individuals

Photocopy the list of assertive rights (page 78) and pin it up in your bedroom, or some other appropriate place and each morning read the list aloud. Alternatively, read the list just before going to sleep – this will help you to memorize it.

After this week, mark the rights you are having difficulty with and choose one of these to work on during the next week. Write this particular right up, in large poster form, and pin it up in a prominent place. Alternatively, write it at the top of each days' page in your diary. At the end of the week check your progress and reward yourself appropriately.

Groups

Divide into pairs. Each person should read the list of rights out to someone, owning each right for themselves. For example: 'I have the right to ask for what I want, realizing that the other person has the right to say "No".' The other person should in some way acknowledge that you have this right. For example they may smile, nod or say something like this: 'Yes, you certainly can ask.'

By doing this, you are positively reinforcing this new value and helping to obliterate the old messages which may still be in your heads, telling you that it is not OK to be assertive.

Super Confidence

See Chapter Six

Exercise 23
Others' rights

Individuals

Note down which rights you have difficulty in respecting in relation to other people. For example:

- **Privacy** – 'I'm nosey.'

- **Success** – 'I find it embarrassing when someone is very open about their achievements.'

- **Assertiveness** – 'I don't like it when my children tell me I'm wrong even if I know they are right.'

- **Independence** – 'I kick up a fuss if my partner wants to spend time alone with his or her friends.'

Think about where your difficulty with this right is rooted. For example, perhaps it was difficult for you to assert it as a child. Perhaps someone in your life is abusing this right for you. Perhaps you are frightened and fearful of losing the other person.

Try to talk over your difficulty and the reason for it with the other people and ask them to help you to change your behaviour, but to be tolerant of you if you do not achieve overnight success.

Groups

Do the above exercise in pairs and set a goal and reward for each other. Each person should share with the rest of the group which rights they have chosen to work on. Say, for example, 'I am going to respect other people's right to privacy.'

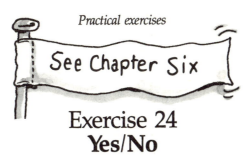

See Chapter Six

Exercise 24
Yes/No

Individuals

Make a list of people – or types of people – to whom you find it difficult to say 'no', without making up elaborate stories or unnecessary justifications. Note down particular situations. For example, 'refusing to help my neighbour for the tenth time this week'; 'declining an invitation to a party'; 'refusing to buy things from salespeople'.

Do the same for your problems in saying 'yes'.

Make a note of your fears and anxieties in relation to each of these situations and beside it put down the rational (Adult) answer. For example:

Fear/anxiety	Rational response
'They may not like me anymore'	'I am a good enough neighbour'
'They may never ask me out again.'	'Well, you can ask them if you really want to.'
'Perhaps I'm not really a caring enough mother. Maybe I am penny-pinching about my children's future life. Supposing he's right and I do die tomorrow? Maybe I should take out an extra policy.'	'My current policy is all I can reasonably afford at the moment.'
'If I agree this time, they'll never leave me alone.'	'I can use the broken record technique.'

Fear/anxiety	Rational response
'If I say "yes" to going to lunch he may think I am going to go to bed with him.'	'You can tell him that you are not!'

Groups

This is a fun exercise with a serious purpose. It is very useful for getting some energy going, if you are all flagging.

Divide into pairs and find a space to stand together in the room. One person is going to simply say 'no' while the other person will simply say 'yes'. The object of the exercise is to win your partner over using non-verbal behaviour to strengthen your case. Experiment with as many voices, gestures, and so on, as you can think of and see which one your partner is most vulnerable to and which ones help you to feel more persistent.

Share in pairs how you were affected in this exercise and talk about your real life difficulties in saying a simple 'yes' or 'no'.

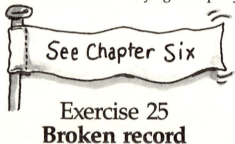

See Chapter Six

Exercise 25
Broken record

Individuals

During the next week, try to find a situation in which you could practise broken record. For example, you may need to return something to a shop; make some other kind of complaint; send your children to bed on time; ask someone to tidy their room.

Make notes on the conversation, recording your feelings as well as the words and the outcome. Note any resistances you may have had to overcome in order to remain persistent. Ask yourself when you were at your most vulnerable. For example, was it when they suggested you had been negligent, or was it when they tried to make you feel sorry for them?

Ask a friend to give you some practice, through role-play, on these areas. Alternatively, practise saying your broken record line (for example, 'I have now been working here very satisfactorily for five years and I would like you to review my salary' or 'I know that you are busy but this coffee is cold and I would like it replaced.') over and over again, in the bath, or in another favourite relaxing place.

Groups

Divide into pairs, or small groups, and, using Broken Record, role-play one of the following situations:

- A salesperson is trying to sell you a shampoo/car/dress/computer/TV which costs more than you wish to pay

- You have won £10,000 on a lottery and have decided how you wish to spend your money. A 'friend' from a charity which you generously support is making a request for some of this money. Your task is to resist.

Divide into small groups. Each person should choose a situation from her own life to role-play, using the broken record technique. Have at least one person observing and supporting the person trying to be assertive and use two people to be the 'nasties' and put on the pressure.

See Chapter Seven

Exercise 26
Small talk

Individuals

Make a list of ten subjects which you could 'safely' talk about to other people – subjects which are not likely to bring up strong feelings in you or other people. For example:

- The weather
- An aspect of your work
- Favourite places to live

- A recent news story
- Your holiday this summer
- Cats

Make a note of a conversation 'opener' you could use for each of these subjects (remembering that it must not be in any way threatening to the other person).

Note down some facts or stories, you know about these subjects and during the next week see if you can add to this store of information.

Find an opportunity to practise your small talk, such as in a bus or supermarket queue, or in the office.

Make sure you reward yourself for your achievements.

Groups

Mill around the room until the leader tells you to stop and find a partner. She then instructs you to talk to each other on a particular subject. Start with very easy subjects such as what you had for tea tonight and then progress to slightly more difficult topics like your favourite way of relaxing, or a recent news story.

Share in pairs how you behaved in this exercise. Did you allow the other person to do most of the talking? Did you talk too much? Which subjects did you find most difficult? Discuss changes you would like to make in your behaviour.

See Chapter Seven

Exercise 27
Initiating conversation

Individuals

During the next week try to initiate at least six conversations with a variety of people. You could do this with strangers or with people you know. Note down your progress and any areas of difficulty. Reward yourself.

Ring a friend and say that you would like to chat for five minutes. Ask if it is a convenient time. If not, can she or he suggest another possible time? (We often wait for some special news before we ring friends; if the news doesn't arrive we get out of contact. Remember, close friendships need nourishing.)

Groups

Make a list of the subjects which you know something about. For example:

- Wild flowers
- Obtaining grants
- Photography
- Teenagers

- Computers
- Holidays in Spain
- Vegetarian cookery
- Yoga.

Put your name at the top of your list. Stick these lists up on the wall and spend five minutes reading each other's lists.

Initiate a series of conversations with people who have listed subjects which are of interest to you.

Divide into pairs to share your experiences during that exercise. Congratulate each other, if congratulations are in order.

See Chapter Seven

Exercise 28
Reflective listening

Individuals

Record several short interviews or conversations from the TV or radio. Play them back several times, noting the way the listener communicated to the talker that she or he was listening and assess whether it was a good, adequate or poor response.

Using these tapes, note down how you could have improved on the quality of the listening responses by using the technique of reflective listening (see page 84).

Groups

Divide into groups of three or four people. Take it in turns to be talkers and listeners and observers. Give the talkers a subject, such as, 'An awful holiday experience'; 'My pet fears' or 'My favourite film star'. The listeners should be instructed to use the technique of reflective listening to encourage the talker.

Observers should feedback to the listeners about their behaviour, remembering to make any criticisms specific and constructive. Listeners should share any difficulties which they may have had. For example, 'When you started to tell me about losing your ticket, it reminded me of the time I lost mine and I felt desperate to interrupt and tell you my story!'; or 'I kept wanting to reassure you that snakes are harmless instead of just letting you talk.'

See Chapter Seven

Exercise 29
Non-verbal communication

Individuals

Spend half-an-hour watching a TV programme, noting down all the body communication you can observe. Note whether these 'messages' were received, understood, acknowledged or ignored. (A video recorder would, of course, make this exercise easier. Otherwise you will have to devise an effective shorthand.)

Note whether you use any or all of these gestures and expressions. During the next week vow to be super-sensitive to all the body signals you are sending out to others. Check whether you are receiving other people's accurately, by asking questions such as: 'I notice you are frowning. Are you worried?'; 'You seem very tense today, am I right?'; or 'I see you are tapping your finger, and I wonder if what I am saying is annoying you?'

Groups

Sit in a circle. Each person should take it in turns to mime an emotion. The rest of the group must guess which emotion you are conveying.

Divide into pairs, and using only facial and hand expression – not words – take it in turns to 'tell' the other person about your weekend. Try to guess what kind of weekend your partner had. Was it happy? Was it sad? Was it boring?

See Chapter Eight

Exercise 30
Reviving the skeletons

Individuals

Make a list of a few 'mini' skeletons which you have lurking in your cupboard – pieces of information about your past, your present life or your attitudes and feelings which very few people know about.

Thinking carefully about these, decide whether it may now be possible to bring some of them out into the daylight. Note the people with whom you would like to share them, and the people with whom you would choose not to share.

Attempt to share at least one of these stories with someone whom you trust during the next week.

Groups

Each person should complete the first part of the above exercise on their own.

In silence, look around the group and decide which are the people with whom you could share your secrets and which are the ones which whom you would have difficulty. Reflect on the reasons for your decision.

Using printing to disguise your handwriting, each person should write a secret on a piece of paper – one which they would be prepared to share anonymously with the group. Put these in a container and give a good mix! Distribute one to each person.

Each person reads the secret which is on their piece of paper and makes a statement which reveals what they guess the person who wrote it might be fearing (that is, about revealing their secret). For example, 'Before I go to bed I have to check that all the plugs have been pulled out. I won't trust anyone else to do it.' 'I guess that this person is worried that people will think she is really weird.' Or, 'When I was 18 years old, I was caught shoplifting but I wasn't charged.' 'I guess this person might be worried that people will not be able to trust her ever again or that she ought to have been punished.' Or, 'Sometimes I feel like running away and deserting my whole family.' 'I guess this person is frightened that people will think that at heart she doesn't love her family and is really a thoroughly selfish person.'

Divide into pairs, choosing to be with someone whom you trust. Reveal one of your secrets to each other and share your anxieties about doing so. If you have been unable to reveal a secret share your feelings about not being able to do so.

See Chapter Seven

Exercise 31
Giving compliments

Individuals

Make a list of people in your life whose personality, behaviour or work you admire. Note down several specific and not general reasons for making these choices. For example, not: 'She's a good mother,' but rather: 'She loves her children and she is happy for them to be different from her. She has rules but she is prepared to negotiate with them.'

During the next week set yourself the task of saying at least three of these comments on your list to the people concerned, even if it means making a special phone call or visit. Don't wait for the golden opportunity – make it happen!

Groups

Each person should jot down one specific character trait, physical attribute or behaviour which they have admired in other group members.

Sit in a circle. Alternate members should move around the group, so that you should each have a chance to share these thoughts assertively with each other.

Divide into pairs and share this experience. Set each other a goal for the next week to give a compliment to someone in your life outside the group.

See Chapter Seven

Exercise 32
Receiving compliments

Individuals

Make a list of some of the compliments you can recall having been given to you. Beside each one, note down a typically unassertive response and a preferred assertive one. For example:

Compliment : 'Your hair looks really good today.'
Unassertive response : 'That's only because I've just combed it!'
Assertive response : 'Thanks, I'm pleased with it as well.'

For the next week make a point of responding assertively to any compliment you may receive. (You should be receiving more by now, just because you are giving more!) Note down any assertive responses you may hear other people give to compliments.

Groups

As a group, make a list on a large sheet of paper of about six compliments which people in the group commonly receive or hear.

Divide into small groups and list as many unassertive responses as you can to these compliments.

Return to the large group and share these. Discuss which

would be the preferable assertive responses.

Divide into pairs. Each person should talk about the influence their childhood had on their ability to receive compliments assertively. For example, 'I wasn't given much practice!' or 'My Mum/Dad could never take a compliment'; or 'I was always teased about blushing.'

Similarly, share any pressures you may be experiencing in your current life which do not help you in relation to receiving compliments. For example, you may be in a relationship in which the other person constantly puts you down, or in a job, the pressure of which sets you up for continual failure.

Each person should receive a compliment from their partner in front of the large group at the end of the session.

See Chapter Seven

Exercise 33
Making requests

Individuals

Make a list of some of the requests you would like to be able to make of people. For example:

- To ask for the music in a restaurant to be turned down

- To ask your mother-in-law to stop giving you advice

- To ask a man for a date

- To ask for a salary rise

- To ask for a reduction in an estimate

- To ask your partner to alter his lovemaking behaviour.

Take each one in turn and note down your rights in each case. These may be legal rights or merely your basic rights as a human being.

Note down any particular cultural 'code' you may wish to respect or acknowledge. For example, the other person may be of a different religion, gender, race or generation.

Script your request, using the tables on page 90 as a guide.

Practise reading your script aloud, into a tape recorder if possible.

Groups

Do the above exercise on your own. Divide into small groups and use role-play to practise making your request.

Divide into pairs and set each other a goal and a reward.

See Chapter Seven

Exercise 34
Public speaking

Individuals

Imagine that you have been asked to make a 15-minute speech on a subject of your choice. Make some clear, concise notes on a series of cards, summarizing what you want to say. Prepare any visual aids you may wish to use.

Note down a few outfits which you have, or would like to have, in your wardrobe, which you could wear for a variety of occasions where you may be required to make a speech. For example, a wedding; office meeting; social club AGM; or a TV broadcast! Think through your reasons for making these choices.

Imagine yourself in one of these outfits (or actually put one on), and proceed to practise delivering your speech in front of a mirror.

If you have been courageous enough to record yourself, replay the tape and be your own critic. Don't forget to congratulate and reward yourself as well as finding faults.

Groups

Make a list of topics suitable for a short speech. For example:

● Television and violence

- Men and sport
- Good and bad parties
- Bringing up children.

Write each one on a separate slip of paper and put these in a container and give a good mix! Each person should take a slip and then have ten minutes in which to prepare a three-minute speech on the topic they have been given.

Take it in turns to stand in front of the group and give your speeches.

Give each other some specific, positive feedback followed by any constructive advice and tips.

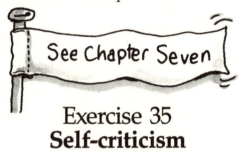

See Chapter Seven

Exercise 35
Self-criticism

Individuals

Write the answer to the following questions:

- Which parts of your body do you find unattractive?

- Is there any other aspect of your 'natural' inheritance which you do not like or are particularly sensitive about (for example, your voice, race, class, intelligence, family)?

- Which of your personality traits would you like to be rid of?

- Which aspects of your behaviour are you not particularly proud of but are content to live with for the time being, at least?

- Have you any faults which you are currently trying to correct?

- Which are the three biggest mistakes you have made in your life?

Remind yourself that you have a right not to be perfect and a right to make mistakes. Do some deep slow breathing and then read this list aloud several times using a strong, even, clear voice, while you are sitting or standing in an assertive position.

Groups

Write the answers to the above questions.

Divide into pairs and read your lists to each other in an assertive manner, remembering your right not to be perfect and to make mistakes. The person listening should merely accept and acknowledge the self-criticisms of their partners, or ask for further clarification. She should not try to rescue or comfort her by such statements as: 'Oh, I've always thought your hair was lovely!'; 'Well, perhaps it was for the best anyway;' 'Gosh, you should see how untidy my desk is!' or 'I like your quiet manner; loud people are horrible.'

Share your feelings about doing this exercise. Was it difficult for you? If so, what was your fear about? Were you frightened that your partner would be shocked or wouldn't like you? Did you as listeners want to rescue the other person? If so, why? Did you feel uncomfortable not being rescued?

Each person should share one self-criticism from their list with the rest of the group.

See Chapter Eight

Exercise 36
Receiving fair criticism

Individuals

Using your self-criticism list as a guide, write down a list of ten criticisms, people could or do make of you which you would agree with.

Write down, beside each, your possible assertive replies, using either fogging or negative assertion or negative enquiry, according to the situation. Remember that many criticisms are disguised as questions or apparently caring comments! For example:

Critic 'You're always tired, aren't you?
Assertive reply 'Yes, I do look tired because I am overworking at the moment.' (Negative assertion.)

Critic 'You let your children walk all over you.'
Assertive reply 'Maybe they do get the upper hand of me sometimes.' (Fogging.)

Critic 'You always get involved with the wrong sort of man.'
Assertive reply 'Do you think I'm generally a bad judge of character?' (Negative enquiry.)

Write a script asking someone who is persistently reminding you of your faults to stop doing so.

Groups

Make a list of criticisms, as in the first part of the above exercise.

Break into small groups. Each person should take it in turns to give their list of criticisms to two people in the group who use this as a guide to being horrible! (Being a critic in a group like this can be the most difficult part of a confidence-building course but it is useful to take this role because it helps to 'demystify' critics, if you have learned to play their 'game'!)

Use assertive strategies (as above) to acknowledge any disguised criticism and to protect yourself. Don't be tempted to justify yourself.

Break into pairs and help each other write a script which you could use to ask someone who is persistently reminding you of your faults to stop doing so.

Each person should read their script out to the rest of the group.

Finish the session by making each person give an assertive compliment to their partner in front of the whole group.

Practical exercises

See Chapter Eight

Exercise 37
Receiving unjust criticism

Individuals

Make a list of a number of criticisms which people have made of you which have been unjust. If your memory fails you, use your imagination!

Using the technique of fogging, write an assertive reply for each criticism. Add a statement, in brackets, which reminds you of the truth but which you do not have to share with the critic. (To do so usually just fuels their fire; fogging on its own is the most effective way of blocking this kind of 'nasty'. Your task here is to protect yourself, stop the put-downs and not to convince your critic that you are right.) For example:

Critic 'You're a typical woman; you are always nagging.'
Assertive response 'Perhaps I do go on a bit.' (I am persistent. I am not a nagger.)

Critic 'You should try harder, it's not that difficult.'
Assertive response 'Maybe you're right. Perhaps it's not that difficult.' (I know that I am doing my best.)

Critic 'You're never on time.'
Assertive response 'Maybe I do have a tendency to be late sometimes.' (I have only been late twice this month and I am trying to improve my timekeeping.)

Write a script, addressing someone who has unfairly criticized you, pointing out their error and asking them, in future, to make their criticisms fair and constructive.

Groups

Each person should complete the first part of the above exercise.

Break into small groups and role-play giving unfair criticisms. As before, use two critics as this makes for better practice and enables the critics to persist a little longer.

Finish by allowing each person to make three of the statements they had put in brackets to the rest of the group. (For example, 'I have only been late for work once this month.')

See Chapter Nine

Exercise 38
The tough interview

Individuals

Imagine that you wish to apply for a new job or a promotion. Make a list of all the tough, critical questions or comments an interviewer could make if she or he saw your CV or application form. Imagine that she or he knows about all your mistakes and failings as well as your strengths. Write an assertive and not apologetic response for each. For example:

Interviewer 'I notice that it has taken you rather a long time to apply for a promotion.'

You 'Yes, I have waited some years before applying. It was important to me to gain a good working knowledge of the shop floor first.'

Interviewer 'I notice that your management experience has been very limited.'

You 'Yes, it is true that my previous posts have not given me much opportunity to use my management potential and that is why I am so keen now to be promoted.

Interviewer 'It seems that you have changed direction many times. Do you have difficulty in making up your mind?'

You 'Yes, you're right that I did spend several years testing out my interests and my aptitudes and this experience gave me an invaluable base of self-knowledge and self-confidence. I certainly am now able to act decisively. For example, . . .'

Practise reading these replies aloud, or better still role-play an interview with a friend.

Groups

Divide into groups of approximately six people. Take it in turns to interview each other. Have a panel of three interviewers. The others in the group should help the interviewee prepare herself for any difficult questions (see the above exercise). Meanwhile the interviewers should prepare themselves. If you have real CVs, use these. If not spend some time preparing some basic information on yourself and your work history to give to the interviewing panel.

The group should give the interviewee some specific constructive criticism. If she had some difficulty, use someone else in the group to role-play the interview, so that she has a chance to view the scene more objectively. It is important to remember that this is not a way of showing the interviewees how they ought to do it, because otherwise their performance will become stilted and they will not be 'themselves'. Run the interview through a third time, with the interviewee taking part. There should be a definite improvement on her performance.

See Chapter Eight

Exercise 39
Anger messages from childhood

Individuals

Write down the answers to the following questions.

● How did your mother (or mother figure) show her anger, frustration or irritation?

● How did your father (or significant father figure) show his negative feelings?

● What did your religion teach you about handling anger?

● Can you remember any of your teachers getting angry? If so, how did they show their feelings?

● What generally happened at home if you became angry?

- What happened at school if you expressed negative feelings such as frustration or irritation?

- As a child, did you ever experience being physically hurt at the hands of someone who was angry?

- What stories or myths can you remember reading, or being told, which contained messages about anger? (What about those horrible giants?)

Summarize the content of these 'messages' in several sentences. For example: 'If women get angry, they may get hurt;' 'It always pays to count to ten;' 'Be careful of men. Don't upset them;' 'The strongest will always win;' 'Always keep the peace if you can;' or 'Anger is sinful and wicked.'

Think carefully about these messages and tick the ones you agree with and cross out the ones with which you disagree.

Groups

Divide into small groups and brainstorm the kind of messages you received in childhood about anger. Make a poster of the questions in the above exercise, if it will help jog some memories.

In the large group, share these messages and discuss whether or not they fit in with your own philosophy.

Divide again into small groups and each write some new messages on large sheets of paper. For example, 'Anger is a natural response to frustration;' 'Stored up anger is dangerous;' 'We have a right to feel angry about injustice.'

Share these in the large group and pin the sheets up around the room. Leave them there during the sessions in which you are working on your anger. You could start each session by reading them out.

See Chapter Eight

Exercise 40
Anger hierarchies

Individuals

Brainstorm as many things as you can think of which make you angry, irritated or frustrated.

Choose ten of these to list in order of the depth of emotion they each engender in you. Name the emotion in brackets which you generally feel about this problem or situation. For example:

- My partner's infidelity
- My boss's refusal to listen to my complaints
- Racism (such as apartheid)
- Sexism (such as the office calendar)
- People smoking in the office
- My mother's advice about the house
- The children not washing up their mugs
- My neighbours' overgrown hedge
- The buses being late
- Litter in the streets.

Beside each, note which of your rights has, or is being, abused.

Choose one situation from the bottom of your list to try to work on during the next week. Set a goal for yourself. For example, you could write a letter to the city council about the litter, or, if you are feeling quite brave, you could try to confront people who you see dropping litter.

Reward yourself.

Each week try to creep a little further up your list, until you feel quite confident and guilt-free about expressing your anger.

Groups

Do the above exercise in pairs, reading out your lists to each other.

Set a goal for each other for the bottom of your lists.

Use role-play to practise expressing irritation to people. You can either use real-life situations from the past or the present, or you can do an imaginary scene. If, for example, someone knows that generally they experience difficulty in expressing irritation to members of their family, you could choose to play a typical scene such as a family meal.

After these kinds of exercises it is sometimes necessary to 'de-role' the people who have played the 'nasties' because it is so easy to absorb some of the feelings and wonder if some of the irritation really belongs to you. There are various ways of 'de-roling', but the simplest and most effective way I have found is simply for the person who played the role to have an opportunity of sharing with the group the ways in which she or he feels she or he differs from the character they have just played. For example:

I'm Jane and, although I know that I do put people down occasionally, this is a behaviour which I do not like and am trying to change. Another difference is that I am willing to admit that I do make mistakes. I also think I am a more caring and understanding person than Gill, the character which I have just played.

In these kinds of role-play it is always important to remember what your goals are. The focus of attention should be on the protagonist's *behaviour*. You should be looking at ways in which you can help her to change her words and her non-verbal communication. You should resist the temptation to play 'amateur psychologist' (in other words, endlessly theorizing about why this is happening) or becoming *too* sympathetic. It is so easy to get into playing the very unproductive game which Eric Berne named 'Ain't it Awful?' In this game, which I am sure we are all guilty of playing from time to time, we stay with the 'safe' option of collectively moaning about the 'nasties', instead of facing up to the more threatening alternative of looking at ways in which we can change the unsatisfactory aspects of our own behaviour!

Practical exercises

See Chapter Eight

Exercise 41
Letting go

Individuals

Complete the sentence 'It's not fair . . .' as many times as you can. For example:

- 'It's not fair that I've too much work to do.'

- 'It's not fair that that I'm expected to be so understanding.'

- 'It's not fair that I have so little money.'

- 'It's not fair that the world is so unjust.'

- 'It's not fair that George treats me like a china doll.'

- 'It's not fair that I haven't got an understanding Mum.'

- 'It's not fair that I always have to do what Joan says.'

Sit on the floor with a big pile of cushions in front of you and read this list out with as loud a voice as your neighbours will stand while at the same time giving your cushions a good thumping. This exercise enables you to get more in contact with your anger and to unlock the energy which you need to use in order to express it. Remember all emotions need physical expression. Using this phrase 'It's not fair' is useful because we associate it with young children who are frustrated and not afraid of letting you know how they are feeling!

During the next few weeks, if you are in any of these situations which you find frustrating, remember your 'It's not fair' statement and the energy which accompanied it. See if you can express this in any way to the person or people concerned. If you judge that it would be unwise to express your feelings either fully or at all, experiment with thumping a cushion when you get home instead. In this way you may not be resolving the problem (some, of course, cannot be resolved) but you are protecting yourself from the negative consequences of pent-up emotions.

Groups

Each person should complete the first part of the above exercise. Break into small groups to complete the second part. Share your experiences.

At the next session, re-form your groups and on this occasion give each person the opportunity to express their feelings about a frustrating situation that has occurred during the past week. An alternative to thumping the cushions can be to kick them around the room or throw them at the wall!

Finish each exercise by doing an assertiveness training role-play, if appropriate. For example, if someone had chosen to look at their relationship with a colleague and had successfully let go of some of her feelings by thumping cushions, set up a scene whereby she can rehearse expressing her feelings to her colleague without causing an office riot or getting the sack!

See Chapter Eight

Exercise 42
Justified anger in an unjust world

Individuals

Buy yourself a selection of newspapers and, as you read them, mark the stories which irritate or infuriate you. Note down any similar themes such as sexism, attacks on children, Third World difficulties.

Select one of these themes to look at. Ask yourself the following questions:

- Am I using my anger constructively?

- Do I share my anger with others over this issue?

- Do I tend to moan and wail about it, and do very little else?

- What could I, realistically, achieve if I used some of the energy in my anger?

- What price would I be prepared to pay in order to achieve it?

- Could I get any support for my actions?

- If I did begin to act, how could I check whether my actions are being effective?

- What effect would success have on my self-esteem and my self-confidence?

Set yourself a realistic goal!

Groups

Do the above exercise in small groups, helping each other to set realistic goals. It may be that one or two people may have similar goals and may want to do a joint project or act as a support to each other.

Share your goals in the large group and agree to report back on your work after a certain period, perhaps three or four weeks.

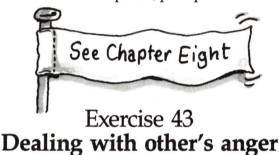

See Chapter Eight

Exercise 43
Dealing with other's anger

Individuals

Recall a scene when someone has been angry with you and you were not happy with the way you behaved in the situation. Work out a script for yourself which could help you deal more assertively with that situation. Answer the following questions:

- What is the other person feeling?

- What am I feeling?

- What statement could I use broken record with in order to get their attention?

- What feedback or information can I ask for?

- How can I ask what it is that the other person wants?

- How can we renegotiate this relationship afterwards, so that this situation does not recur again?

- Is it appropriate for me to apologize?

Read your script through several times. Lie in a relaxed position, with your eyes closed, and take yourself in your mind to that scene. Imagine yourself feeling calm and in control, using your script in that same situation.

Groups

Do the first part of the above exercise in pairs, helping each other to prepare a script.

Divide into small groups and role-play the problem scene, so that each person has a chance to use their script and practise behaving assertively. (This exercise is also helpful for releasing the energy of our own anger; it is often easier to get angry on someone else's behalf!)

See Chapter Nine

Exercise 44
Family relationships

Individuals

List the members of your family with whom you feel a link, either positively or negatively.

Select the same number of buttons, coins or other small objects. Choose one to represent you and place that in the centre of a table. Using the other objects to represent other family members, place them around you in a pattern which is representative of their relationship with you and each other. For example:

Looking at these patterns, assess whether they are satisfactory to you. Imagining that you could be as confident as you would like to be, how different would this pattern be? Move your objects to the positions you would like to see them in.

Replace the objects in their real positions and decide upon one realistic move which you could make if you changed your behaviour slightly. For example, you might be able to move closer to your father if you began to express more positive feelings towards him or you might not feel so dependent on your sister if you could make some more friends.

Note whether, if you make this move, this will have a 'knock-on' effect on your relationships with other family members. Be aware of the consequences of this possible effect and judge whether it is affecting your decision. For example, getting closer to father may mean that your relationship with sister may change. Are you prepared for the change? How will you meet any challenge to your new behaviour?

Do this exercise at regular intervals and draw a rough diagram as a record. If you are changing behaviour you should certainly see some movement in your family relationship patterns. If there is no movement, then perhaps you are playing too safe!

Groups

Do the first part of the above exercise on your own.

Take it in turns to use other group members, rather than objects, to make up a sculpted picture of your family relationships.

Imagining yourself to be super-confident, move the people to the positions you would like to see them in, being aware of the 'knock-on' effect as discussed above.

Standing behind each person who is representing a member of your family, imagine that you are in their shoes and say what you think of this new behaviour and the new relationships. For example, you may have moved yourself a little further away from your mother because if you were as confident as you would like to be, you would feel less obliged to visit her so often. So you might, as mother, say: 'Oh dear, I do miss Jane. I am going to be very lonely. I don't know how I will be able to cope,' or 'Thank goodness Jane seems more capable of standing on her own two feet now. At last Bill and I can have a Christmas on our own.'

When you have completed this part of the exercise, move to the front of your sculpture. Each person playing a member of your family should say what you have just said when you were 'in their shoes'. You must then answer them assertively, without over-justifying your actions.

Everyone should share the feelings and thoughts which may have arisen out of doing your own sculpture or watching or participating in the other sculptures.

In pairs set each other realistic goals in relation to changing your pattern of family relationships.

See Chapter Nine

Exercise 45
Friendships

Individuals

Select several relationships with women who are important to you and which you consider to be friendships. Using the guide on page 109 as a checklist, note down any aspects of the relationships you wish to change.

Identify any rights which may be being abused by either of you. Make a note of the aspects of your own behaviour which you would like to alter. For example:

● 'I would like to tell Sharon how much I value my friendship with her and why I respect her so much.'

● 'I would like to see more of John and less of Rita.'

● 'I would like to be able to tell Gill that I find her gossip distasteful.'

● 'I would like to be able to ask Jean to take more notice of my needs.'

Choosing just one of these aspects, write out a script for yourself to use when you next meet. For example, 'Jean, for the last few months, we seem to have spent all our time together talking about your problems at work. (*Explanation*). I am beginning to feel resentful, and whilst I appreciate that you are under a lot of stress (*Feelings*), I would like you to show an interest in what is happening in my life (*Needs*), and then I will feel less like 'switching off' the minute you bring up your problems (*Consequences*).'

Note down what you would be prepared to do if your friends do not like the new 'confident you'.

Groups

Each person should complete the first part of the exercise on their own.

Get into pairs and share your lists. Help each other set a goal and do a script (see above).

Use role-play to rehearse your scripts.

See Chapter Nine

Exercise 46
Authority figures

Individuals

Make a list of all the authority figures with whom you experience difficulty and note down a typical situation. For example:

- Asking a doctor to clarify an aspect of diagnosis or treatment

- Asking your boss to consider changing an unsatisfactory procedure

- Asking your bank manager for a loan

- Making a complaint to a senior manager

- Obtaining information from your children's headteacher

- Asking for help from your tutor.

Analyse the reason for your anxiety and fear and note whether it is rational or irrational. If the latter, try to understand what 'old messages' may be affecting your right to be assertive. For example, perhaps your mother was very obsequious to doctors, or your father would have disapproved of your loan, or perhaps you had an ogre of a headteacher when you were at school.

Lie in a comfortable position, close your eyes and imagine someone you know and judge to be a confident person. In your mind's eye take that person into the situation with which you are experiencing difficulty. 'Watch' how they would cope with the same situation.

Write yourself some scripts and practise reading them aloud.

Set a goal for yourself to use one of these scripts by the end of the month. Don't forget to plan your reward as well!

Groups

Brainstorm some of the authority figures with which you are experiencing difficulties.

In small groups share how these problems may have originated, for example, experiences in your childhood or a particular trauma.

Using role-play, take it in turns to try different assertive approaches to some of the key figures on your list, such as doctors, headmasters and bosses.

In pairs, discuss which of these approaches would be most useful to you and give each other a chance to practise.

Set each other a realistic goal.

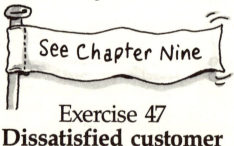

See Chapter Nine

Exercise 47
Dissatisfied customer

Individuals

Think of some of the times when you have received less than satisfactory service, but you have decided not to complain because 'it wasn't worth it'. For example:

● Cold food in a restaurant

- Uncaring attitude of doctor's receptionist
- Persistent delays on the railway
- Short change in a shop
- No heating in a bus
- Imperfect goods
- Forgetful solicitor
- Patronizing doctor
- Uncommunicative headteacher.

Write down an assertive complaint for each of these, using, perhaps the skills of broken record and scripting.

Practise saying these aloud in front of a mirror, so that you can check that you are also using assertive body language. Beside each note how you would reward yourself if you used any of these on a future occasion. Remember that complaining about these more 'minor' irritations is good practice for the more serious stuff and, of course, if enough people complain something is usually done!

Groups

Brainstorm some examples (such as those listed above) of unsatisfactory service.

Break into small groups and, using role play, practise some assertive strategies for making reasonable complaints. Each group should take a different scenario.

Each small group demonstrates to the others a scene which illustrates how to make an assertive complaint.

Break into pairs and set yourselves a goal regarding making a complaint for the next week or month.

Exercise 48
Relating to your lover

Individuals

Write down some of the messages you have in your head about
sex. These may include old ones which are around and you
would prefer eradicated! For example:

- 'I am not a very sexy person.'

- 'Sex is embarrassing.'

- 'Sex is a necessary evil.'

- 'Men get more pleasure out of sex.'

- 'Very few women can have orgasms.'

- 'Sex isn't as important as friendship.'

- 'You should want sex. You're odd if you don't.'

- 'You can't read about it; it's something you just know about.'

- 'It's natural for men to initiate.'

Beside each, give the authors of these messages, for example,
'mother', 'the nuns at school', 'my husband', etc. Cross out the
ones you wish to keep and insert any others you may wish to
add.

Think about your sex education. Was it adequate? (Most
women I see were given little or no information.) If not, buy
yourself, or borrow, a good book. If you still feel you need
guidance, go to an advisory service.

Make a list of the changes you would like in your relationship
with your partner.

Write yourself a script and vow to use it!

Groups

Brainstorm your rights as women with regard to your sexual relationships.

On your own, check your relationship against these rights and the guide on page 112.

Discuss, in pairs, if you feel able to do so. If not, share in the large group the right you are going to stop denying yourself within your sexual relationship. For example, 'I have a right not to know about something or to understand' or 'I have a right to ask for something, realizing that the other person has the right to say "no" '.

See Chapter Nine

Exercise 49
Relating to children

Individuals

Make a list of the problems you experience in relating to children. For example:

- 'I am not very good at disciplining them and I cannot keep order.'

- 'I cannot be spontaneous with them. I feel silly playing games with them.'

- 'They bring out the bossy side of me.'

- 'I spoil them. They can get anything out of me.'

- 'I feel uncomfortable when they want a cuddle.'

- 'I worry all the time about them.'

- 'I never know what they're feeling. They don't seem to confide in me.'

Take each problem and counsel yourself about it. Absolve yourself of some of the guilt by trying to understand the reasons for your difficulty. For example:

- 'I am afraid of going over the top and becoming like my father.'·

- 'No one played with me very much when I was little.'

- 'I'm so powerless at work and in my marriage. I can only get power for myself when I am with children.'

Note any fear and anxiety you may be experiencing uncon-sciously in each situation, for example, 'I am frightened that they will not love me.' Check whether it is rational or not.

Use your knowledge of Transactional Analysis (pages 48-60) to help you understand which part of your personality you may need to develop in order to feel more confident with children. For example, you may want to develop your Free Child and you could do this by joining a drama class where there are oppor-tunities to do improvisations or join a free movement class. Alternatively, you may want to develop your Nurturing Parent, so you could join a massage class or do some voluntary work. Or perhaps you wish to be more Adult, so you may join a class in parenting skills or buy a book on child development.

If the children concerned are old enough, consider whether you could discuss your difficulties with them. Children really respect adults who can admit that they are not perfect and they can be remarkably understanding if you explain the reasons for your difficulty.

Set yourself a realistic goal and share this with the children, if appropriate.

Groups

Do the first section of the above exercise.

Break into pairs and counsel each other. First, try to find the reasons for the difficulties and second, a solution.

Use role-play to work on any specific problems. Working through the following list would be good practice for anyone!

- Sending unwilling children to bed

- Resisting the temptation to buy an ice-cream

- Getting order in an unruly class

- Confronting bullies

- Dealing with a temper tantrum in a supermarket

● Confronting a child about an unsatisfactory school report.

Share some fun games which you know, and end your session by having some fun playing a couple of them!

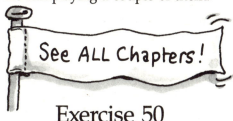

See ALL Chapters!

Exercise 50
Evaluation of your progress

Individuals and groups

Answer the following questions on a separate piece of paper when you have completed your confidence-building course. You can then assess how much progress you have made and whether you need to do any further work. In view of the fact that this evaluation may be done in a group, I have not used scales or percentages because confidence-building should never be regarded as a competitive game.

1 List as many signs of confident behaviour as you can.
2 How do people become confident?
3 List some of the special difficulties for women in our society.
4 How can behaviour patterns be changed?
5 List some of the factors in your own personal life which have affected your confidence.
6 List some examples of your Parent behaviour.
7 List some examples of your Adult behaviour.
8 List some examples of your Child behaviour.
9 Which part of your personality still needs further development?
10 List six of your strengths.
11 List six of your weaknesses.
12 Are you able to share your strengths and weaknesses more easily with people now?
13 List six ways in which you have looked after yourself during the last month.
14 Can you give examples of ways in which you are still not looking after yourself?

15 List three of your achievements over the last month.
16 Have you shared any of these with anyone? If so, whom?
17 List six characteristics of aggressive behaviour.
18 List six characteristics of passive behaviour.
19 List six characteristics of assertive behaviour.
20 List two examples of situations of each behaviour which you have used appropriately during the last month.
21 How many of the assertive rights can you remember?
22 Describe the technique of Broken Record.
23 Quote an example of when you have successfully used it.
24 Name some important negotiating skills.
25 Have you recently developed your negotiating skills?
26 Name some important points about the art of conversation.
27 Give an example of an assertive compliment which you have given during the past week.
28 Name some important points to remember about receiving compliments.
29 List two examples of assertive requests which you have made during the last month.
30 Name three topics about which you feel you would be prepared to speak in public.
31 Name some important points to remember when giving a public speech.
32 Describe the technique of fogging and give an example.
33 Describe the technique of negative assertion and give an example.
34 Describe the technique of negative enquiry and give an example.
35 List some of the rules for giving criticism.
36 List some of the rules for receiving criticism.
37 What is healing anger?
38 What is destructive anger?
39 Give examples of two situations in which you have expressed your frustration or anger, during the past month.
40 Give examples of three changes you have made in your relationships since the beginning of this course.
41 Give examples of changes you still would like to make.

Your future action plan

1 Now that you have completed this questionnaire, assess which areas you still need to develop with regard to becoming as confident as you would like to be.
2 Prioritize this list.
3 Note what action you need to take over the next six months.
4 Note what you hope to achieve if you follow this action plan.

Further reading

Assertiveness training

Sharon and Gordon Bower, *Asserting Yourself* (Addison-Wesley Publishing, USA, 1976).
Anne Dickson, *A Woman in Your Own Right* (Quartet Books, 1982).
Herbert Feensterheim and Jean Baer, *Don't Say Yes When You Want to Say No* (Futura, 1975).
Gael Lindenfield, *Assert Yourself* (Thorsons, 1987).
Stanlee Phelps and Nancy Austin, *The Assertive Woman* (Arlington Books, 1988).
Manuel J. Smith, *When I Say No I Feel Guilty* (Bantam, 1975).
David Stubbs, *Assertiveness at Work* (Pan Books, 1985).

Transactional Analysis

Eric Berne, *Games People Play,* (Penguin, 1970).
Eric Berne, *What Do You Say After You Say Hello?* (Corgi, 1975).
John Dusay, *Egograms* (Bantam, 1977).
Thomas Harris, *I'm OK – You're OK* (Pan, 1970).
Thomas and Amy Harris, *Staying OK* (Pan, 1985).
Muriel James and Dorothy Jongeward, *Born to Win* (Addison-Wesley, USA, 1985).
Muriel James and Dorothy Jongeward, *The People Book* (Addison-Wesley, USA, 1975).

Games books for groups

Donna Brandes and Howard Phillips, *Gamester's Handbook* (Hutchinson, 1977).
Donna Brandes, *Gamester's Handbook Two* (Hutchinson, 1982).
Sheila Ernst and Lucy Goodison, *In Our Own Hands* (The Women's Press, 1981).
Sue Jennings, *Creative Drama in Groupwork* (Winslow Press, 1986).
Anna Scher and Charles Verrall, *100+ Ideas for Drama* (Heinemann, 1975).

Guides to counselling and therapy

Lindsay Knight, *Talking to a Stranger* (Fontana, 1986).
Joel Kovel, *A Complete Guide to Therapy* (Penguin, 1978).

Miscellaneous books of interest

Michael Argyle, *The Psychology of Happiness* (Methuen, 1987).
Colette Dowling, *The Cinderella Complex* (Pocket Books, 1981).
Robin Norwood, *Women Who Love Too Much* (Arrow Books, 1985).
Dorothy Rowe, *Beyond Fear* (Fontana, 1987).
Virginia Satir, *Peoplemaking* (Souvenir Press, 1978).
Gail Sheehy, *Pathfinders* (Bantam 1981).
Robin Skynner and John Cleese, *Families and How to Survive Them* (Methuen, 1983).
Philip Zimbardo, *Shyness* (Pan Books, 1981).

Taking it further

If you want to join a confidence-building or assertiveness course there are a number of ways you can find out who holds them and where they are run.

- Contact the reference section of your local public library. They will have a list of courses with contact names and addresses.

- If you live in a town with a university or college in it, the Psychology Department there may either run courses itself or be able to put you in touch with other people in your area who do.

- Some of the large teaching hospitals run courses which you may find helpful, but you may find there is a waiting list for these or you need a referral from a health practitioner.

- You could try contacting assertiveness training courses through your local women's group, if you have one, or through adverts on the noticeboard of health food shops, although you might want to check these out thoroughly before you commit yourself long term.

Index

Figures in **bold** refer to practical exercises.